COMMAND AT SCALE

THE SYSTEM THAT CONTROLS PERFORMANCE

MICHAEL HOLLINGSWORTH

First Edition

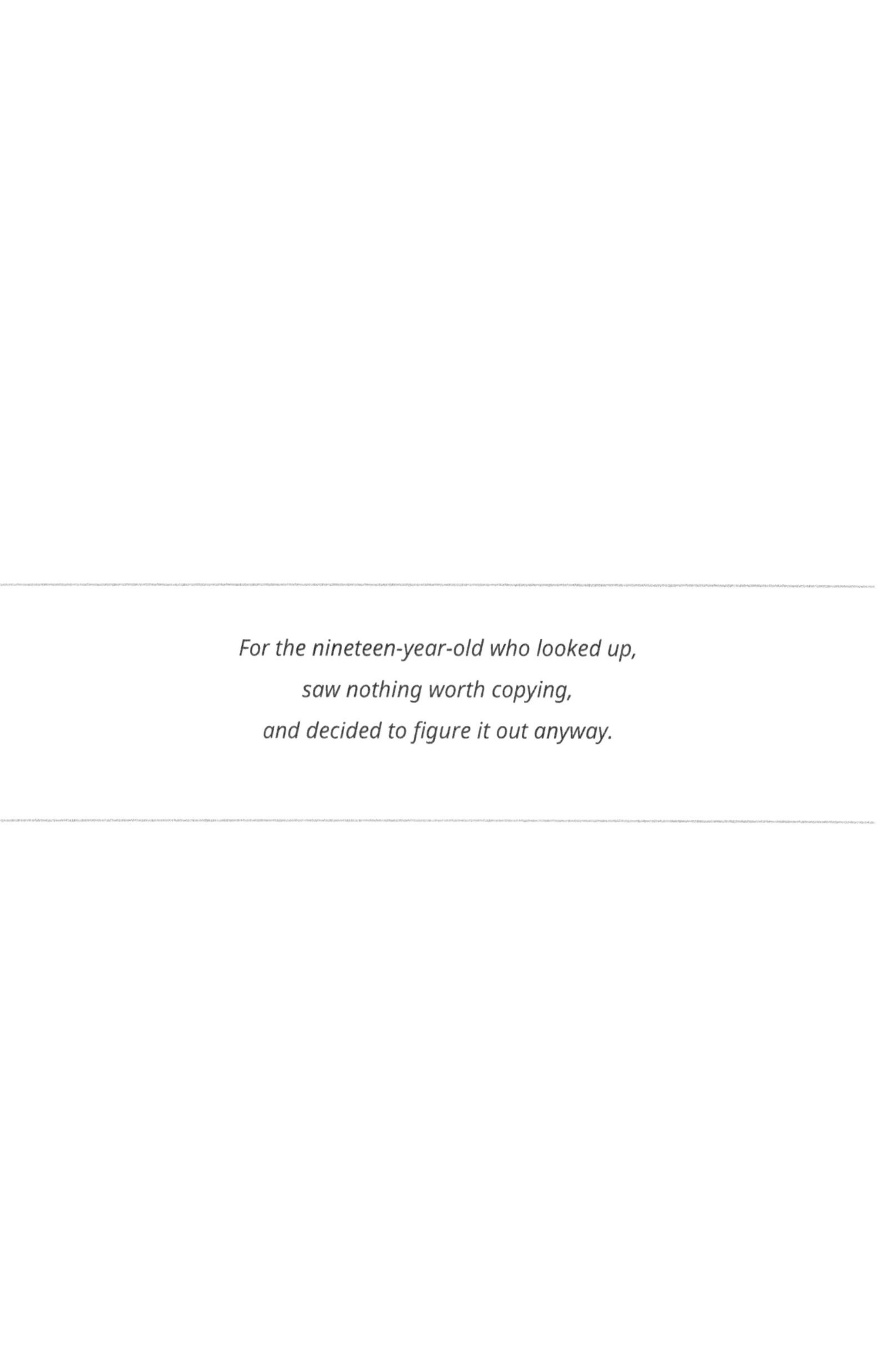

For the nineteen-year-old who looked up,
saw nothing worth copying,
and decided to figure it out anyway.

TABLE OF CONTENTS

How to Use This Book 4
Who This Book Is For 5
Foreword—I Had No Blueprint 7
Introduction 10
PART I—COMMAND: The Mindset and Identity 15
1. This Is Not a Leadership Book 15
2. Standards, Not Speeches 17
3. The System Commander Identity 21
4. Operator vs. Leader vs. System Commander 27
5. The Standard on Paper 31
6. Operations Don't Care What You Say 35
PART II—CONTROL: From Effort to System 38
7. Learning the Hard Way 38
8. The Repeating Miss 41
9. Nightly Failure, System Fix 44
PART III—SCALE: Ownership, Accountability, and Command 50
10. The Promotion Problem 50
11. The Hero Trap: Ownership Over Heroics 54
12. Clarity + Accountability = Control 57
13. Accountability at Scale 61
PART IV—EXECUTE: Living as a System Commander 67
14. The Real Job of a Leader 67
15. The System Commander Daily Audit 71
16. The Identity Test 76
17. Command in Any Operation 79
18. Building a Bench of System Commanders 82
PART V—TRANSFORM: Your First 30 Days 89
19. Your First 30 Days as a System Commander 89
20. The Leader You're Building Toward 101
Glossary 104
What Comes Next 107
APPENDICES
A—The Control System Readiness Assessment 108
B—The 12-Week Command at Scale Program 111
C—The System Commander Creed 117
D—Laws of Command 118
About the Author 120

HOW TO USE THIS BOOK

A Note Before You Start

This book is designed to be read straight through once—then used as a reference. The first read gives you the full framework. You will see how each part connects: standards lead to checks, checks lead to accountability, accountability leads to ownership, ownership leads to command. Read it in order the first time so the system makes sense as a whole.

After that, use it as a field guide. Each chapter is self-contained. If you are dealing with a specific problem—repeated misses, accountability gaps, a team that will not hold standard without you—go directly to the chapter that addresses it.

FOR FASTEST RESULTS

- Read Part I (Chapters 1–6) to establish your identity as a System Commander.
- Start your 30-Day Plan (Chapter 19) within 24 hours of finishing the book.
- Use Appendix A to assess your operation before and after.
- Work through Appendix B to begin the full 12-week build.
- Use Appendix C as a daily reminder of who you are building toward.
- Keep Appendices B, C, and D nearby—they are your build tools, your identity reminder, and your operating principles. Return to them often.

One final note: reading this book will not change your operation. Installing the system will. The difference between leaders who transform their operations and those who don't is not understanding—it is action.

> ***"Read it. Then go build it."***

WHO THIS BOOK IS FOR

This Book Was Written for You

This book was not written for executives in corner offices. It was not written for consultants, theorists, or people who talk about leadership from a stage.

It was written for the person who runs things.

The operations manager who arrives before the team and leaves after them. The operations director who personally catches every problem no one else caught. The department head who carries the whole floor on their back—and wonders why nothing holds when they step away.

> ***"If you are tired of being the only thing standing between your operation and chaos—this book is for you."***

You will find this book useful if:

> You are an operations manager, general manager, or multi-unit operator responsible for daily execution at scale.

> You are a mid-level or senior leader inside a large organization—retail, logistics, healthcare, hospitality, or any environment where performance has to hold across shifts, locations, and teams.

> You are a department head, team lead, or supervisor who has been given authority but no real system for producing consistent results.

> You have read leadership books before and felt like they were written for a different kind of problem than the one you're actually living.

> You are high-performing but dependent—your operation runs because you run it, and you know that is not sustainable.

This book does not require a business degree, a corporate budget, or permission from anyone above you. It requires a decision: to stop managing chaos and start building control.

If you are ready to make that decision, turn the page.

FOREWORD

I Had No Blueprint

I was nineteen years old when I stepped into my first salaried leadership role.

No one sat me down and explained what leadership actually was. No one handed me a framework or a system or a set of principles to operate from. I was handed a title, a set of keys, and an expectation: figure it out.

So I did what most young leaders do. I looked up.

I watched the people above me. The managers, the directors, the leaders who had been doing this for ten, fifteen, twenty years. I watched how they moved through their days, how they handled problems, how they ran their teams.

And what I saw changed me.

Not because it was inspiring. Because it wasn't.

> ***"Every leader above me operated without urgency. Without precision. Without any real drive to solve problems at speed."***

They were smart people. Experienced people. People who had built careers in leadership. But when I watched them operate, I didn't see leaders. I saw people managing the day. Surviving the shift. Holding the title without filling the role.

They weren't bad people. They were placeholders.

And that realization—at nineteen, watching people twice my age drift through leadership roles that could have been so much more—became the engine behind everything I've built since.

What Drives Uncommon Leaders

Most people find their motivation in admiration. They see someone doing something remarkable and they think: "I want to be like that."

My motivation came from the opposite direction.

I looked at the leadership around me and thought: "I refuse to be like that."

That refusal—quiet at first, then louder every year—drove me to study execution obsessively. To look for what actually produced results, not just what looked like leadership from a distance. To build systems when everyone else was having conversations. To enforce standards when everyone else was writing reminders.

I became convinced of something early, and fifteen years of operating have only confirmed it:

The majority of people in leadership roles are not leading. They are occupying a position. They are doing enough to keep the title. They are managing the appearance of effort.

The few who operate differently—the System Commanders—are running circles around them. Not because they work harder. Because they work differently. They build control instead of chasing compliance. They design systems instead of repeating instructions. They move fast and decide clearly while everyone else is still scheduling a meeting about the problem.

Why I Wrote This Book

I wrote this book because I wish someone had handed it to me at nineteen.

It would have saved me years. It would have saved me the exhaustion of trying to lead through effort alone—of carrying operations on my own energy until I was empty. It would have shown me earlier what I had to learn the hard way: that the goal is not to be needed. The goal is to build something that doesn't need you to survive.

That is command at scale. And it is learnable.

You don't have to be born with it. You don't have to stumble into it after a decade of mistakes. It is a system. And systems can be installed.

That is what this book is here to do.

What This System Produced

I did not develop these principles in a classroom. I developed them over fifteen years of running large-scale retail operations—stores with hundreds of employees, multi-million-dollar weekly volumes, and performance standards that had to hold across every shift whether I was there or not.

Here is what installing a real control system produced in my operations:

RESULTS

- Eliminated the same recurring misses that had been documented for months—in under 30 days—by changing the system, not the people.
- Built supervisors who ran the floor to standard without waiting for direction. My presence became confirmation, not requirement.
- Reduced floor dependency to the point where my operation held standard during full-day absences—no calls, no check-ins, no fires.
- Developed team members who went on to lead their own operations using the same framework. The system replicated itself.
- Moved from Operator mode—personally catching every miss—to System Commander mode: designing the environment that catches misses automatically.

None of this required a bigger team, more budget, or a different workforce. It required a different system.

The people I led were not the problem. The system I was running them through was.

> ***"Fix the system. The people will follow."***

INTRODUCTION

The System That Controls Performance

The first thing you notice about a parking lot in February is the wind. Not the cold exactly—you get used to that—but the way the wind cuts across forty thousand square feet of open asphalt with nothing to stop it. No walls. No roof. Just you, the cart corral, and however many carts customers left wherever they felt like leaving them that day. Some were in the corral. Most weren't. A few were against a curb on the far end of the lot where someone had shoved them rather than walk the extra sixty feet. A couple were tipped over near the cart return, spun sideways by the same wind that was currently working its way through every gap in the jacket I'd bought with my first check.

I was seventeen. That was my job. Go get the carts.

I did it in heat and in rain and in the kind of cold where your fingers stop bending right and you're moving carts by leaning into them with your forearms. I did it when the lot was full and the lines were backed up into the main drive and customers sat in their cars with their blinkers on waiting for a space, blocking anyone trying to leave. I learned every corner of that lot. I learned which corrals filled up first, which areas customers ignored, where the carts would drift if you didn't lock the wheels. I learned the lot the way you learn anything—by being in it, every day, with no one checking on you.

What I didn't understand then, but understand completely now, was what the parking lot was actually telling me.

When there were no carts at the door, customers came in frustrated. They'd already started their trip irritated—they'd carried their child through a busy parking lot, unaware they needed to grab a cart before entering—and once inside, faced with no carts available, they were left to either wait for someone to finish using one or go back outside to find one. They came through the door already behind. And the people who should have been thinking about that—the people with the titles and the offices and the clipboards—were inside. Not managing what was actually happening. Managing the appearance of managing.

I'd come in from a cart run, hands barely working, and I'd see them standing near the service desk or walking the floor with a deliberate look on their face, the look that said they were engaged. I'd mention the lot—not confrontationally, just as a fact. The carts were bunched up on the south end. There were twelve carts backed against the garden center entrance. The corral by the main entrance was overflowing. And I'd get one of a few responses. "Okay, thanks." Or: "We're working on it." Or, my personal favorite, a slow nod that meant the information had been received and would be forgotten before I made it back outside.

It took me a while to name what I was seeing. I was a teenager, a cart pusher—not a leadership theorist. But somewhere in those hours of working a problem that nobody with authority seemed to actually want to solve, I started to understand something no training program ever taught me directly: the operation doesn't reflect what leaders say. It reflects what they allow. Every day that lot told the truth—not the version of the truth that got written in the shift notes or described in the morning huddle, but the actual truth you could walk out and see with your eyes. And if you were paying attention, the lot told you just as much about the leadership inside the building as it did about cart coverage outside it.

That is the thing about operations. They expose you. You can write the values on the wall. You can run the meeting, say the right words, and genuinely mean them. But the operation is running twenty-four hours a day. It will tell your team—and your customers, and anyone paying attention—exactly what you enforce. Exactly what you let slide. Exactly where your standards stop being standards and start being suggestions. You cannot hide from it. You can only manage it—or pretend you are, while the lot fills up.

I spent years climbing from that parking lot into roles that gave me the authority to fix the problems I used to only point at. And I can tell you that the fundamental problem has never changed. It is not a staffing problem. It is not a training problem. It is not a technology problem. It is a standards problem. Specifically: there is a gap between the standard that exists on paper or in a manager's head and the standard being delivered at floor level right now, while you are doing something else.

The parking lot is still the test. Whatever your operation is—wherever your standards are either held or abandoned—that is your parking lot. The carts are either at the door or they aren't. The zone is either recovered or it isn't. The handoff either happened or it didn't. And the operation is telling the truth about you, clearly and continuously, whether you are out there listening or not.

This book is about closing that gap. Not with motivation. Not with culture initiatives or vision statements. With a system. With standards written down, assigned to names, verified at specific times, and enforced without exception. That is the work. It is not complicated. It is not glamorous. And most of the people who should be doing it are inside the building right now, not listening.

That recognition—specific, grinding, unglamorous—is what this book is about. Not the drama of a crisis. Not a turnaround story. The quiet, daily truth that most leaders in high-volume operations never say out loud: the system only works when I am standing in it. The second I leave, it degrades. I am not a leader. I am a load-bearing wall. Remove me, and the structure collapses.

> ***"That is not command. That is dependency. The difference between the two is specific, learnable, and installable. This book will teach you that difference—not as a concept to reflect on, but as a system to install."***

What This Book Actually Is

Most leadership books are written to inspire. They are collections of principles, stories, and frameworks designed to make you feel differently about leadership. This book is not written to change how you feel. It is written to change what you install.

Think of it as an installation guide. When you finish a chapter, there is something concrete to put in place—a standard, a protocol, a system mechanism. By the time you finish the book, you will have a complete operational control framework: a method for setting standards that hold, a structure for accountability that does not depend on your mood or availability, and a cadence for correction that prevents small performance gaps from becoming permanent behavioral norms. You will not just have ideas to consider. You will have a framework to run.

The Three Laws of Command

Every system built from this book rests on three laws. They are not motivational slogans. They are operational principles—statements about how organizations actually behave, derived from observation, not aspiration. Before you read the rest of this book, you need to understand these three laws at a level deeper than agreement. Most leaders will read them and nod. That is not enough. You need to read them and then look at your operation and ask: Where is the evidence of this right now, today, on my floor?

The laws are not comfortable. The first one—that what you tolerate becomes the standard—implicates you directly. Not your team. You. The second law removes the escape route of having said something without following through. The third law eliminates the fiction that certain performance failures are inevitable or beyond your control. Together, these three laws shift accountability squarely onto the leader's structure and behavior. That is where it belongs.

THREE LAWS OF COMMAND

1. What you tolerate becomes the standard.
2. If behavior does not change, leadership did not happen.
3. Repeated problems are not random—they are allowed.

These three laws are the foundation of every principle in this book. You will find the complete Laws of Command—all fifteen—in Appendix D. Keep them close.

> ***"When you leave the floor, the system holds. That is command at scale."***

PART I

Command: The Mindset and Identity

I

CHAPTER 1

This Is Not a Leadership Book

> ***"If your operation only works when you are watching, you don't have leadership. You have dependency."***

And dependency breaks under pressure.

Walk into any bookstore and you will find hundreds of leadership books. Books about vision, values, communication, and culture. Books that tell you to be more present, more empathetic, more strategic, more inspirational.

There is nothing wrong with those ideas. But they are not what most struggling leaders need.

Most struggling leaders do not need more inspiration. They need a system that works when they are not standing over it. They need control.

The Problem With Inspiration

Inspiration is temporary. A great speech motivates people for a morning. A powerful vision gets buy-in during a meeting. But when that meeting ends and people return to their stations—what determines performance is not what was said. It is what is expected, measured, and enforced.

A team that performs because it was inspired is a team that depends on being re-inspired constantly. The leader becomes the engine. The moment the engine stops, performance stops.

That is dependency. And dependency is the enemy of scale.

A team that performs because there is a clear standard, an ownership structure, and a real consequence for falling short—that team performs when the leader is absent. When the leader is in a meeting. When the leader takes a day off. That is control. And control is the goal of this book.

What This Book Will Teach You

THIS BOOK WILL TEACH YOU

- How to define standards so clearly that no one can misinterpret them
- How to install checks that catch problems before they become habits
- How to enforce accountability the moment it's needed
- How to assign ownership so nothing falls through the cracks
- How to build a bench of leaders who think and operate the way you do

LAW—THE CONTROL TEST

"Does your operation hold standard when you are not there? If the answer is no—you don't have a leadership problem. You have a systems problem."

That distinction matters. Because fixing a systems problem looks very different from trying to fix a "people problem." People problems get you into conversations, performance reviews, and endless coaching cycles. Systems problems get you into design mode. You stop asking "What is wrong with this person?" and start asking "What is wrong with this system?"

LESSON

Leadership is measured by what holds in your absence—not by what you accomplish while present.

CHAPTER 2

Standards, Not Speeches

> ***"What you tolerate becomes the standard."***

This is the most important sentence in this book. Read it again.

What you tolerate becomes the standard.

Not what you say. Not what you want. Not what you write on a whiteboard or post on a break room wall. What you tolerate. What you walk past. What you acknowledge and then let slide.

Your real standards are not written anywhere. They are lived every day in the gaps between what you say and what you allow.

The Speech Trap

The default response when performance falls short is a speech. A meeting gets called. Expectations are restated. The manager walks away feeling like something was addressed. Nothing was addressed.

A speech is information transfer. It tells people what you think the standard should be. But it does nothing to enforce it. And enforcement—not communication—is what changes behavior.

The team leaves the meeting and returns to their patterns. Because the patterns were never disrupted. The system that allowed the problem was never redesigned. Next week, the same meeting happens again. And the week after that.

Standards Are Enforced in Moments

The standard in any operation is set not in meetings, but in moments. Specifically, in the moments when a leader sees a miss and decides—consciously or not—whether to address it.

Every time you walk past a problem without addressing it, you publish the standard: this is acceptable here.

Every time you stop, correct it, and follow through—you publish a different standard: this is not acceptable here.

CASE STUDY // CART BAY COLLAPSE

Saturday. Peak hours.
Cars stacking. Customers circling. Frustration rising.
Cart bay empty. Everyone sees it. No one moves.

A leader walks out. Looks. Pauses.
"We're always behind..."
Walks away.

That moment set the standard. Not through instruction. Through inaction.
The team learned: empty cart bays are fine here.
And that became the norm—not because anyone decided it, but because no one stopped it.

Writing Real Standards

"Keep the floor clean." That is a preference, not a standard.

"All aisles clear of product by 9:00 AM and 4:00 PM, verified by the shift lead." That is a standard.

Real standards are specific, measurable, time-bound, and owned by one person. When you write them that way, enforcement becomes simple. The standard is either met or it is not. There is no debate.

> LAW—THE STANDARD LAW
>
> *"What you tolerate becomes the standard. Every time. Without exception."*

Writing the standard is the easy part. The hard part begins the moment the standard is tested—and it will be tested, almost always within forty-eight hours. A new standard enters an operation carrying a question the team has asked about every previous standard: Is this one real? They are not asking it consciously. They are watching. The team has seen posted standards before. They have seen binders updated and forgotten. They have seen a manager announce a new expectation on Monday and stop mentioning it by Wednesday. The standard is not assessed by what it says. It is assessed by what happens when someone does not follow it.

The first miss is not a disciplinary event. It is an inflection point. When a team member misses the new standard within its first two days—leaves the station unstocked, skips the sign-off, completes the process out of sequence—the leader faces a moment that carries more weight than the standard itself. Every person within line of sight of that interaction is reading the outcome. If the leader addresses it directly and immediately, the standard gains credibility. If the leader notices it, says nothing, and moves on, the standard has been reclassified.

It is now a suggestion. Suggestions do not run operations.

What closes the gap between written standard and lived standard is not follow-up—it is first enforcement. One firm, visible, professional correction in the first forty-eight hours does more for compliance than thirty days of reminders. The team is not making decisions about behavior based on the words in the standard. They are making decisions based on what they have observed to be the real consequence of deviation. First enforcement sets that observation. It tells the team: this manager is different from the last one; this expectation has weight. The cost of this correction on the leader's end is low. The cost of skipping it compounds.

A leader who lets the first miss slide has not posted a standard. They have posted a suggestion with a lamination. The lamination communicates effort—which is real—but effort without enforcement is only evidence that the leader cared enough to write it down. Operations are not run by what leaders care about. They are run by what leaders act on. The standard becomes real through enforcement—and the first enforcement moment is disproportionately powerful precisely because it is first. After that moment, the standard's authority either exists or it does not. What happens next will simply confirm which.

> LESSON
>
> *Standards are enforced in moments, not meetings.*

CHAPTER 3

The System Commander Identity

Identity drives behavior. Who you believe yourself to be determines how you act under pressure, when no one is watching, when it would be easier to let something slide.

Most people in leadership roles carry one of three identities—even if they have never named them. They are an Operator, a Leader, or a System Commander. Operators show up, complete tasks, and survive the day. Leaders identify problems, create solutions, and drive execution. System Commanders build systems, scale performance, and develop other leaders.

A SYSTEM COMMANDER

- Sets the standard with precision
- Enforces the standard without negotiation
- Relies on systems, not personal effort
- Moves fast and decides clearly
- Builds structures that make their own constant presence unnecessary

System Commanders do not manage people. They manage conditions. They design environments in which performance is the default—not the exception.

The Speed Principle

One of the defining traits of a System Commander is speed. Not recklessness—decisiveness. Slow leaders create ambiguity. When a problem is identified but not immediately addressed, the team interprets the delay as tolerance. Fast leaders control the narrative. When a miss is addressed within minutes rather than days, the team learns the standard is real.

The identity trap is not a motivation problem. Most leaders who read this framework will recognize themselves somewhere in the Operator-to-Leader-to-System Commander continuum, make a private commitment, and then walk back into their operation and default to the exact behavior they acknowledged was holding them back. This is not hypocrisy—it is the predictable result of identity pressure. When a standard breaks visibly, when the team is short, when a new manager is struggling in real time, the pressure to act personally is enormous because personal action is fast, visible, and immediately rewarding. It produces the sensation of leadership. The problem is that the sensation of leadership is not the same as its function.

Identity is not claimed. It is demonstrated—and demonstrated most clearly under conditions that make the old identity easier than the new one. A leader can call themselves a System Commander in every planning session and every one-on-one. None of that self-designation matters. The honest test is what your operation reflects when you are not in the room. If standards hold without you, the identity is real. If they degrade the moment you step out, the title is aspirational, not actual.

The transition from Leader to System Commander is the hardest shift in this framework—not because it requires more skill, but because it requires resisting a pull that feels virtuous. Leaders who built their reputations on personal competence are being asked to stop doing the thing they are most rewarded for. That is not an intellectual problem; it is a behavioral one, reinforced constantly. A manager who personally recovers a chaotic shift gets thanked and recognized. A System Commander who builds conditions that prevent chaotic shifts entirely gets neither the drama nor the credit. The operation runs. The System Commander identity is most effective precisely when it is least visible, and that invisibility makes the transition difficult to sustain.

What the System Commander identity looks like in practice is a series of specific choices at specific pressure points. When a standard breaks—a process is being skipped, a position is uncovered, a metric falls below floor—the Operator grabs it personally. The Leader corrects it on the spot. The System Commander asks one question before acting: does my system have a mechanism to catch this without me? If yes, the mechanism is activated. If no, the response is to build that mechanism, not to be the mechanism. Every moment you become the mechanism, you confirm to yourself and your team that the system does not have to hold—because you will.

When a new manager is struggling, the System Commander's role is not to perform the work more competently. It is to determine whether the manager has the documented standard, the coaching structure, and the defined consequence framework needed to develop. If those conditions are absent, the failure belongs to the system. Building those conditions is the work. Doing the manager's job for them delays both their development and the operation's maturity.

The choice at each of these moments is not between action and inaction. It is between two kinds of action. One builds the operation's dependence on you. The other builds its independence from you. The System Commander identity is the commitment to choose the second one, consistently enough that it stops being a choice.

The Identity Trap

There is a specific reason the shift from Operator to System Commander is hard, and it has nothing to do with skill. Most managers who have been in operations long enough already understand the theory. They can explain leverage. They can draw the org chart. They know, intellectually, that a system that runs without them is more valuable than a manager who keeps showing up to hold things together.

They revert anyway. The reason is not knowledge. It is reward architecture.

The leadership reward system is wired backward for System Commanders.

When you personally save a shift—jump on a register, pull freight at midnight, cover a no-call—you get immediate positive feedback. The team thanks you. Your manager sees you. You feel like a leader. That reward is real and immediate. It lands in your body the same way any positive reinforcement lands: you feel useful, you are recognized, and the situation improves because of something you did directly. Your brain logs this as a successful leadership behavior and files it under "do this again."

The problem is what it is actually rewarding: the system's failure to function without you. Every hero moment is a data point confirming that the system is broken and you are the patch. You are being praised for the exact thing holding your operation back. The recognition feels like success. It is a signal of failure dressed in approval.

This is not a character flaw. It is a feedback loop. And as long as that loop runs, the system will not get built—because the behavior the system requires you to stop is the behavior that keeps getting reinforced.

When the system works, nothing happens. No one calls. No one thanks you. No one notices.

When freight finishes on time because the process was designed correctly; when the team handles a coverage gap without escalating it to you; when a new manager resolves a customer issue independently because the escalation threshold was clear enough that they knew what to do—the operation runs. Quietly. Without you.

This is why so many leaders intellectually commit to building systems and then emotionally revert to heroism under pressure. The feedback loops are not equal. Heroism produces immediate, personal, social reward. Systemic leadership produces silence. Understanding this asymmetry is not about motivation—it is about recognizing when your brain is steering you toward the rewarded behavior instead of the effective one. You are not weak when you step in to fix something. You are responding to a reinforcement system that was never designed with System Commander leadership in mind.

The trap has a specific texture. It does not announce itself.

It usually starts with a legitimate emergency—a real gap in coverage, a real operational breakdown that genuinely needed your intervention. You stepped in. Things improved. The team was grateful. You were the right person in the right place at the right time. Nothing about that first intervention was wrong.

What happens next is the trap.

Quietly, the same emergency starts happening more often. Not because the team is getting worse—because the system learned that emergencies get your personal attention, and that your personal attention produces results faster than the standard process does. The team is not manipulating you consciously. They are responding rationally to the incentive structure you built by being the hero the first ten times. You created the demand by meeting it.

Each time you step in as the mechanism, you confirm to your team that the system does not have to hold—because you will. And once that belief takes root, you are not leading a system anymore. You are the system. The operation runs on your personal presence, your personal decisions, your personal hours. You have not built leverage.

You have built dependency—and it is running in both directions.

The Exit

There is only one exit from the hero trap, and it is not willpower.

Willpower is the wrong tool because the problem is structural, not motivational. Telling yourself to stop rescuing while the rescue still produces the only positive feedback in the environment is not a strategy—it is a commitment to suffering the same failure in a different mood.

The exit is structural. You must build a system that works well enough that your personal intervention produces a worse long-term outcome than letting the system run. This means writing the standard for the exact situation you keep rescuing. Installing the check that catches the problem before it becomes a rescue. Defining the consequence that makes the system real without you in the room.

Those first few times—when you watch something go wrong and hold yourself back from fixing it personally—it will feel like failure. The team will look at you. You will look at the operation. Every instinct trained by years of being the person who steps up will push you toward the register, the freight cart, the coverage gap. That resistance is not weakness. It is the exact moment the system either gets built or does not.

Leaders who build it are the ones who stayed in the discomfort long enough for the system to respond. They let it be uncomfortable. They wrote the standard afterward instead of jumping in during the crisis. They treated the breakdown as information instead of a personal obligation. Over time, the breakdowns grew fewer. Not because they got better at heroism—because they stopped making heroism the answer.

The system does not get built in the moments you step in. It gets built in the moments you don't.

> LESSON
>
> *You do not rise to the level of your goals. You fall to the level of your systems. Build the system first.*

CHAPTER 4

Operator vs. Leader vs. System Commander

Most operations are not failing because of bad people. They are failing because of misidentified roles. The manager on the floor believes they are leading. The team believes they are being managed. And the operation keeps breaking in the same places, on the same shifts, for the same reasons—because no one has been honest about what identity is actually running the room.

There are three identities available to anyone in a leadership role. They are not levels of a hierarchy. They are not stages you graduate through on a fixed timeline. They are distinct orientations—each with its own logic, its own set of instincts, and its own set of consequences for the operation it governs. Understanding the difference between them is not an academic exercise. It is a diagnostic. Once you can name which identity is running your operation, you can begin to change it.

The Operator

The Operator solves the problem in front of them. They are fast, capable, and deeply familiar with the work. When something breaks, the Operator moves toward it. When a position is uncovered, the Operator fills it. When the freight is behind, the Operator grabs a box. The floor responds to them immediately, because they are the most competent person on it.

The Operator is valuable. In the right role—as a senior team member, a specialist, a floater—Operator-level competence is exactly what the operation needs. The problem is not the identity. The problem is when an Operator is placed in a leadership role and never transitions out of it. An Operator in a leadership title is a high performer who is slowly building a system that cannot function without them.

The Operator's operation looks good when they are present. It looks different when they are not. This is the first diagnostic: walk your floor on a day you are not scheduled. What held? What drifted? Whatever drifted is the gap between your competence and your system. That gap is your real job.

The Leader

The Leader has made the first transition. They have moved from doing the work to directing the work. They communicate priorities. They develop people. They solve problems by identifying root causes and driving corrective action. They are, in most organizations, what a good manager looks like.

The Leader's operation performs based on the quality of their leadership in the moment. Standards hold when the Leader is present and engaged. Team members perform well under the Leader's direction and recognize when the Leader is invested in their development. Performance is relationship-dependent—the better the relationship, the better the output from that individual.

The limitation of the Leader identity is scalability. A Leader can manage a team of eight or twelve well. They can hold relationships tight enough that each individual performs. But as the operation grows, as the team turns over, as the Leader is promoted or transferred, the performance does not transfer with them. The standards existed in the Leader's communication style, not in a documented system. The relationships existed between specific people, not between roles. When the Leader leaves, the operation does not have a system. It has a vacancy.

The System Commander

The System Commander has made the second transition. They have moved from directing the work to engineering the conditions in which the work produces consistent outcomes regardless of who is performing it. The System Commander does not ask "How do I fix this?" They ask "Why did the system allow this to happen, and how do I close that gap?"

The System Commander's operation performs based on the quality of its design. Standards hold because they are documented, trained, checked, and enforced through a consequence structure that functions independent of any single relationship. Performance is not relationship-dependent—it is system-dependent.

The team does not perform because they like their manager. They perform because the environment makes performance the path of least resistance.

This does not mean the System Commander is cold or disconnected. The best System Commanders are often deeply respected by their teams—not because they are liked, but because they are consistent. The team always knows where they stand. The standard never changes based on mood, relationship, or circumstance. That consistency is a form of respect that Leaders who operate on personality can rarely match.

THE THREE-IDENTITY DIAGNOSTIC

Ask yourself these three questions after your next shift:

1. Did I personally fix something today that a system should have caught?
YES / NO

2. Did any standard hold today only because I was present?
YES / NO

3. Did I communicate something today that isn't written down anywhere?
YES / NO

Every YES is Operator or Leader behavior. Every NO is System Commander behavior.

The ratio tells you where you are.

Why the Transition Is Hard

The transition from Leader to System Commander is not blocked by skill. Most experienced operations leaders already have the knowledge required to build a functioning control system. They understand standards. They understand accountability. They understand that a well-designed process beats a well-intended conversation every time.

The reward architecture problem is covered in depth in Chapter 3. The short version: heroism gets recognized; system-building gets silence. Understanding that asymmetry is what makes the transition legible—and a problem you can name is a problem you can solve.

The leaders who make the transition successfully do so by redefining what success feels like. They stop measuring themselves by how many fires they put out and start measuring themselves by how few fires start. The quieter the shift, the better they built. The less they were needed, the more they succeeded. That reorientation is the real work—not the system-building itself, but the identity shift required to believe the system is the point.

> LESSON
>
> *An Operator solves the problem. A Leader addresses the person. A System Commander closes the gap that made the problem possible.*

CHAPTER 5

The Standard on Paper

Most written standards in operations are not standards. They are intentions recorded in standard-shaped language. "Keep the area clean." "Ensure customer satisfaction." "Maintain proper inventory levels." These statements feel like standards when you write them. They sound operational. They look right in a binder or on a laminated card near the break room. The problem is that they cannot be enforced because they cannot be measured. The reason they cannot be measured is that they do not describe an observable outcome—they describe a general direction. Two different employees can read "keep the area clean" and produce entirely different results. Neither can be told with certainty that they were wrong. When a standard permits two different outcomes, it is not a standard. It is an aspiration. And aspiration is not a system.

This is where most operational breakdowns begin. Not on the floor. Not with the team. On paper—or in the absence of paper entirely—when someone in a leadership role accepted vague language in place of precision, and then spent the next six months confused about why the result was inconsistent. You cannot enforce what you cannot define. You cannot define what you cannot describe. And if you cannot describe the outcome in terms that can be observed, photographed, or measured by a second person who was not present, you have not yet written the standard.

A standard that can actually be enforced has four components. Every one of them must be present. Remove any one and the standard degrades back into intention.

The first component is the specific observable behavior—what "done" looks like, described in terms that can be seen, not felt. Not "clean and organized" but every facing full, floor clear of debris, end caps reset. Not "properly stocked" but shelf tags present and aligned, items fronted to the edge, no gaps in the planogram. The test is simple: can someone walk up to this area and determine in sixty seconds whether the standard has been met, without asking anyone? If the answer is no, the behavior is not specific enough.

The second component is the owner. One name. Not a role, not a department, not "the team." One person whose name is attached to the result before the shift begins. Shared ownership is the operational equivalent of no ownership. When three people are responsible for a thing, the first one assumes one of the others handled it, the second one does the same, and the third one finds out at 9:50 PM that nobody did. Assign one name. That person may delegate the execution, but they cannot delegate the accountability.

The third component is the deadline. A specific time—not "end of shift," not "as needed," not "before close." A number. 9:45 PM. 7:00 AM. 2:30 PM. Vague deadlines function as no deadlines. When the completion window is open-ended, completion migrates toward never, and the person responsible has a built-in explanation: "I was going to get to it." A specific time eliminates that excuse. Either it was done by 9:45 or it was not.

The fourth component is the verification method—how the leader confirms the standard was met, by whom, at what time, and what documentation is produced. This is the component most often omitted because it requires the leader to do something, not just the team. Verification is what separates a standard from a request. Without it, the standard is theoretical. The leader either checks it or hopes for it, and hoping is not managing.

Two examples show the difference between a standard written as intention and a standard written to be enforced.

Example A: Zone Recovery

Vague version: "Zoning should be recovered before close."

This fails every component. There is no observable description of what "recovered" means—one person facing the shelves, another sweeping the floor, a third pushing a cart through and calling it done. There is no owner—"zoning" is collective, and collective responsibility dissolves under any pressure. There is no specific time—"before close" is a range, not a deadline, and will be interpreted liberally by whoever is most tired. And there is no verification—no one is checking, no one is documenting, and when the opening team walks into a wrecked floor, there is no record of who was responsible and no way to hold anyone accountable with precision.

Precise version: "Zone 4 (grocery, aisles 12-18) fully recovered—all facings full, aisles clear of debris, end caps reset—by 9:45 PM. Owner: [name]. Verified by floor lead at 9:50 PM with photo documentation to shift log."

This version can be checked. Someone shows up at 9:50, walks the zone, looks at the specific criteria, and either confirms completion or documents the gap. The owner's name is on it before the shift starts, not assigned after something goes wrong. The time is a number, not a window. And the photo in the shift log creates a record that removes every ambiguity about what was done and when.

Example B: Shift Handoff

Vague version: "Make sure the incoming team knows what's going on."

This fails identically. "What's going on" is undefined—one supervisor gives a thirty-second verbal summary, another writes three paragraphs in a notebook no one reads, a third has a fifteen-minute conversation in the parking lot that never makes it to anyone else on the incoming team. No owner is named—the outgoing "team" is responsible, which means no individual is. No time exists—"make sure" implies before they leave, but the window is elastic. And verification is absent entirely. If the incoming supervisor missed something critical because the handoff was incomplete, there is no record of what was communicated, no confirmation it happened, and no accountability for the gap.

Precise version: "Shift handoff summary completed in the shift log by the closing manager by 9:55 PM. Log entry must include: open tasks and current status, department-level staffing gaps for incoming shift, any unresolved customer or operational issues, and inventory actions pending. Opening manager confirms receipt in the log by 10:05 PM. Verified by closing manager before departure."

Now both parties are named. Both have specific times. The content of the handoff is defined—not "what's going on" but four specific categories that cover the operational ground every incoming leader needs. And confirmation is required in both directions, creating a record of the exchange that can be reviewed if something falls through.

Pull three standards from your operation right now. Written ones if they exist. Verbal ones if they do not—write them down first, exactly as you would say them to your team. Then apply the four-component test to each. Is the behavior specific and observable? Is there one named owner? Is there a specific deadline? Is there a documented verification method?

Count how many pass all four components. Every failure is a standards problem—a performance gap built into the system before anyone showed up for their shift. Fix the standard on paper first. Then see what the floor looks like.

> LESSON
>
> *A vague standard is not a standard. It is a permission slip for inconsistency. If two people can read it and reach different conclusions, it is not done yet.*

CHAPTER 6

Operations Don't Care What You Say

Every operation has an honest readout. Not the version that appears in reports or morning huddles—the one that is visible the moment you stop looking with a manager's eyes and start looking with a customer's.

> ***"Operations don't care what you say. They expose what you allow."***

The honest readout of a standard is what's happening on the floor right now, while you're doing something else. Not what was communicated at the last team meeting. Not what the checklist says was completed. What is actually occurring, in real time, when no one with authority is standing over it.

The Honest Readout

Walk your operation with fresh eyes—not with a manager's eyes, but with a customer's eyes. What do you see? What is the real standard?

The honest readout is not comfortable. It reveals not what the team is failing to do—but what the leader has been failing to enforce.

None of what you find is a people problem. It is a standard problem. A system problem. And it is fixable. Your operation is an honest portrait of your standards. If you do not like the portrait, change the standards.

I did not have language for it back then. But I understood the concept. You cannot look at a broken operation and conclude that the people are the problem. People behave exactly as their system allows them to behave. If the system allows drift, there will be drift. If the system produces accountability, there will be accountability.

The condition of the floor is not a reflection of the team. It is a reflection of the leader who decided what the team would be held to.

Experience teaches one consistent truth about leader self-perception: every operations manager believes they are closer to the floor than they actually are. They review the numbers. They do a walk-through. They have conversations with team leads. All of this creates a feeling of proximity that is not the same as operational visibility. Familiarity is the enemy of seeing. When you have walked the same floor enough times, your brain stops registering what is there and starts playing back what is expected. You are no longer seeing the operation. You are confirming a mental model. The gap between that model and actual conditions is where operational drift lives—and it grows in direct proportion to how long you have stopped genuinely looking.

The correction is not complicated, but it requires deliberate effort. Walk in through the customer entrance. Stand in the positions your team stands in for four-hour stretches. Read the flow of the operation from the ground up—from the first point of contact toward the back, not from your office outward. Ask what is confusing, not what is wrong. Ask what slows the work down, not what metrics are underperforming. What you find when you do this is not what your dashboard says. It is the actual operation: the workaround your team invented three weeks ago because the official process broke, the bottleneck everyone has learned to route around, the expectation that was written down but never resourced. The parking lot taught me that honest information does not flow upward on its own. You have to go get it from the ground.

> LESSON
>
> *The floor never lies. What it shows you when you are not expecting it is the real standard—not the one you wrote, but the one you enforced.*

PART II

Control: From Effort to System

CHAPTER 7

Learning the Hard Way

At nineteen, learning through failure, I eventually hit the one insight that changed everything: you cannot lead through effort alone.

I worked harder than anyone around me. I stayed longer. I communicated constantly. I addressed every problem I could see. And nothing was changing. Not in any lasting way.

> ***"I couldn't find a model above me worth following. So I built one."***

That decision—to stop waiting for answers from above and start building from first principles—is the inflection point this entire book is built around. And it starts with one uncomfortable diagnosis: effort is not a system.

The Illusion of Effort

The first trap I fell into was confusing activity with progress. I was doing more than anyone. I was moving constantly, communicating endlessly, present and visible and vocal.

And nothing was changing.

Presence is not leadership. Talking is not leadership.

Leadership is change. It is the measurable movement of behavior from one point to another. If behavior doesn't change, leadership didn't happen—regardless of how much effort went into the attempt.

What No One Told Me

No one told me that standards must be defined before they can be enforced. No one told me that accountability requires consequence. No one told me that repeated problems are system failures, not character flaws.

I had to learn all of it through failure. Through the frustration of saying the same thing thirty times and seeing no change. Through the exhaustion of trying to carry an operation on my own energy.

This book is an attempt to give you what I had to earn the hard way.

> LESSON
>
> *The hard way teaches what the easy way hides. But you don't have to take the hard way if you start with the right system.*

The First System

The first real system I built was not complicated. It was a check. A specific time, a specific person, a specific question: is this done? That was it. Not a process map. Not a performance framework. One scheduled moment where someone confirmed whether a standard had been met—and a defined response if it had not.

It sounds small. The result was not. Problems that had been repeating for months stopped within two weeks. Not because the team changed—because someone was now checking, every time, at the same point in the shift, and the team knew it. The behavior adjusted to the expectation because the expectation was now real. The expectation was verified. It had teeth.

That experience reset something fundamental in how I understood leadership. Every conversation I had before that check existed was effort spent managing symptoms. The check addressed the structure. One structural fix did more than months of individual corrections. I spent the next several years asking one question about every problem I encountered: where is the check that catches this before it becomes a problem? If no check existed, that was the work. Not the conversation. Not the coaching session. The check.

CHAPTER 8

The Repeating Miss

> ***"If behavior doesn't change, leadership didn't happen."***

This is the hardest truth in operational leadership. Because it shifts the responsibility entirely to the leader.

When someone on your team misses the standard, the instinct is to address it with them—coach them, correct them, remind them. And often, that works. Once. The behavior improves, briefly. Then it reverts. And the cycle starts again.

CASE STUDY // THE REPEATING MISS

One associate. Same task. Same miss. Every day.

Manager: "Why isn't this done?"
Associate: "I'll get to it."

Next day. Same conversation. Day after that. Same conversation.

Not because the associate didn't care.
Because nothing happened when they didn't do it.
No consequence. No urgency. No shift in conditions.

The manager kept addressing the symptom.
They never fixed the system that allowed the symptom to persist.

The Real Problem With Repetition

Repetition without consequence is noise. When a leader addresses a miss and no consequence follows, the team learns two things: the standard is negotiable, and the leader's words do not mean much.

Leaders repeat themselves because repetition is more comfortable than consequence, and that comfort has a precise shape. The conversation feels productive—it establishes that the leader noticed, that the leader cares, that the standard is known. There is a social transaction happening. The associate acknowledges the miss, the leader feels heard, and both parties walk away having discharged something. But nothing has changed, and nothing will. The conversation is not a mechanism. It is a ritual functioning as a substitute for a system.

Addressing the symptom repeatedly is the path of least resistance, not the effective one. It requires no documentation, no formal process, no written record, no difficult conversation with an HR partner. It requires only the willingness to say the same thing one more time. Most leaders have an aversion to consequence because consequence feels punitive, and they want to be the kind of leader people work hard for rather than fear. That instinct is not wrong in principle—fear-based compliance is fragile. But when that aversion prevents a leader from building a consistent consequence structure, it does not protect the team. It protects the leader from discomfort at the team's expense.

When a miss repeats, the first diagnostic is not about the person who missed—it is about the system. Three questions asked in sequence will locate the actual failure. Is the standard written, specific, and accessible to the person responsible? Most leaders can answer yes; most operations have some documentation. Is the check scheduled—is there a defined mechanism and cadence confirming execution before the miss becomes visible? Leaders can sometimes answer yes, though the check may lack a clear owner or produce no reviewed record. The third question ends the diagnostic almost every time: is the consequence defined in advance, known to the associate, and applied consistently on every occurrence? Almost no operation can answer yes. Consequence gets handled case by case, shaped by how the leader feels that day, how busy the operation is, how much history exists with the associate. Case-by-case consequence is not consequence. It is judgment, and judgment is not a system.

The cost of this is not contained to the individual being repeatedly addressed. Every other person on the team watches that pattern and makes the same calculation: the standard has been missed multiple times, and the only result has been another conversation. The rational conclusion is that the standard is negotiable. That conclusion does not stay isolated—it spreads across the operation in small calibrations, adjustments made without drama or announcement, as team members absorb the actual signal the leader is sending. The associate who keeps missing is the visible symptom. The degraded operating standard across the entire team is the real consequence. Rebuilding that signal, once sent six times, is substantially harder than building the consequence structure before the repetition begins.

SYSTEM COMMANDER RESPONSE TO A MISS

"This is the standard. It's missed. Fix it now."

No emotion. No lecture. No delay.

Immediate. Clear. Final.

Then: check back within the hour.

Not to catch them failing—to confirm the standard was met.

LAW—THE CHANGE LAW

"If behavior doesn't change, leadership didn't happen. Look first at the system—not the person."

LESSON

Stop repeating yourself. Start building consequences. Repetition without consequence is noise.

CHAPTER 9

Nightly Failure, System Fix

Most leaders discover problems at the moment they become undeniable. The freight is not finished at close. The count is wrong at audit. The line is backed up at peak. They walk into the failure already in progress—and at that point, every option available to them is a reaction. They raise their voice. They pull in bodies from other departments. They tell the team to move faster. It feels like leadership because it is loud and urgent and everyone responds to it. But none of that is leadership. That is crisis management with a leadership costume on.

The verbal directive—"move faster," "get it done," "pick up the pace"—is not a system. It is noise that the team learns to absorb and then ignore. It has no structure. It produces no information. It identifies no constraint. If freight is consistently finishing late, telling people to move faster does not answer the only question that matters: Why is it finishing late? That answer is almost never about effort—the problem is almost always upstream: a receiving window that opens too late, a crew that does not know what is coming before the truck arrives, no intermediate checkpoint that would surface a shortfall before it becomes a catastrophe. The verbal directive skips over all of that and goes straight to blame.

This is the structural difference between urgency and system design. Urgency responds to what is visible right now. System design responds to what makes the visible outcome inevitable. A leader who only operates in urgency mode is a leader who will have the same conversation every single night, because they have done nothing to alter the conditions that produce the failure. The team hears it. The team dreads it. And the team also knows, consciously or not, that the problem will be back tomorrow.

The concept of the pre-deadline check changes the entire logic of operations. Catching a freight shortfall 90 minutes before the close deadline is not the same act as catching it at deadline. At 90 minutes out, options exist. You can reallocate labor.

You can triage by priority zone. You can call a decision about what gets finished and what gets pushed to morning with a plan for morning. At deadline, none of that is available. All you can do is tell people to move faster—and then watch it fail again anyway.

Pre-deadline checks are not instinctive. No one naturally stops mid-freight-push to ask whether they are on pace. That behavior has to be designed into the shift. It requires a check-in point at a specific time, a specific pace metric to evaluate against, and a specific person responsible for calling it. Without that structure, the check-in does not happen. Without the check-in, leaders are guaranteed to arrive at the end of the night and react to a failure they had every opportunity to prevent. The problem was never the team's speed. The problem was a system that provided no early warning—and a leader who mistook their reaction to the alarm for the act of leadership itself.

CASE STUDY // NIGHTLY FAILURE

Freight finished late every night. Every single night.

The leader's response: "They need to move faster."
The team's response: work faster for a day, then revert.

The real problem:
- No defined completion time
- No mid-shift check to catch early warning signs
- No consequence when the standard was missed

"Move faster" was not a system. It was a hope.

The System Fix

FREIGHT COMPLETION SYSTEM

- Standard: "Freight done by 9:00 PM."
- Check: Manager checks at 7:30 PM—if behind pace: immediate intervention.
- Consequence: Missed standard = next-day debrief + root cause.
- Ownership: One team lead owns freight completion per shift.

Within two weeks, late freight disappeared—not because the team changed, but because the system changed. The 7:30 check was the critical piece. It created a 90-minute window to catch a problem while there was still time to correct it.

> LESSON
>
> *The check is not about distrust. It is about design. Build the catch before the miss becomes a habit.*

PART II—REFLECTION QUESTIONS

Control: From Effort to System

Part II exposes the most dangerous trap in operations leadership: the belief that working hard is the same as building control. Effort without system design is just accelerated chaos. This section demands you stop confusing motion with progress and start asking why the same failures keep finding you.

1. Name a miss in your operation that has happened more than twice in the last 90 days. What exactly did you do after the first occurrence? If the answer is "coached the person," you have not solved the problem—you have managed a symptom. What is the actual system failure underneath it?

2. Walk through your nightly failure case: what does the end of your worst operational day look like? What breaks first, what breaks second, and what does your team do when it does? If you cannot answer that in detail, you have not designed for failure—you have only hoped against it.

3. Are you reacting to your operation or designing it? List the last five major decisions you made. How many were in response to a problem that already existed versus a structure you built to prevent a problem from occurring?

4. What is the most expensive recurring mistake in your operation right now—in time, money, or morale? How long has it been recurring? What is the specific moment in your process where the system breaks down and why has it not been addressed?

5. Think about the last time you redesigned a process rather than re-coached a person. If it has been more than 60 days, your default setting is people-management, not system design. What process most urgently needs to be rebuilt rather than re-explained?

6. What does your operation do when you are not physically present to catch errors? Is there a documented process, or is there a cultural understanding that things run looser when you are gone? Those are not the same thing.

7. Identify the point in your weekly cadence where the most chaos is generated. Is that chaos predictable? If it is predictable and you have not designed a system to contain it, why not?

CLOSING CHALLENGE—PART II

- Do not take pride in how hard you work inside a broken system.
- A System Commander's job is not to outrun the chaos—it is to make chaos structurally impossible.
- Every recurring miss is a system gap you have not yet closed. Close it now.

PART III

Scale:
Ownership, Accountability, and Command

CHAPTER 10

The Promotion Problem

Most leaders do not fail at the bottom. They fail after promotion. Because the skills that got them promoted are not the skills their new role requires.

THE PROMOTION GAP

- Execution: "I'll get it done."
- Leadership: "It gets done without me."
- That gap—between doing and enabling—is where most promoted leaders break.

The newly promoted leader knows how to execute. So when their team underperforms, their instinct is to jump in and do it themselves. It is faster, it is better, and it feels like leadership. It is not. It teaches the team: "When things get hard, the manager handles it."

Organizations rarely train people for the actual work of leadership before promoting them. They identify high performers, elevate them, and assume the skills will transfer. The skills do not.

LAW—THE PROMOTION LAW

"Hero leaders get promoted and then trapped. System Commanders get promoted and then freed."

LESSON

The goal after promotion is not to be the best performer on the team. It is to build the conditions in which the team performs without you.

Why Organizations Fail Promoted Leaders

Promotion on performance is rational—you want someone who has demonstrated results in a controlled scope to take on greater responsibility. The error is in what gets assumed to transfer automatically with the promotion: the belief that because someone executed at a high level, they will know how to lead others executing at a high level.

These are not the same skill. They do not share the same cognitive machinery. Performance is about executing a defined task with precision and consistency. Leadership is about designing conditions in which other people execute defined tasks with precision and consistency. One is a doing skill. The other is an architecture skill. Organizations almost universally promote the doing skill and then measure the newly promoted leader against the architecture skill without ever teaching the architecture.

The result is a leader who is competent and lost simultaneously. They know how to work the operation—they were excellent at it. They do not yet know how to command it. Because the organization gave them a title without giving them a framework, they default to what they know: doing the work themselves. This is not a character failure in the promoted leader. It is an institutional design failure. But the promoted leader is the one who pays the price—in stalled performance, in team frustration, in the slow erosion of credibility that comes from holding authority without yet holding command.

The Three Behaviors That Reveal a Promotion Problem

You can identify a leader who has not yet made the transition by watching for three specific behaviors. These are not character defects. They are structural tells.

Behavior One: The leader is the most active person on the floor. Newly promoted leaders often outwork everyone around them. This looks like dedication. What it actually signals is that the leader does not yet trust the system or the team to produce without direct involvement. When your best performer is the leader, the team is not performing. The leader is.

Behavior Two: The leader's decisions are inconsistent based on who is asking. An Operator-turned-leader without a framework makes judgment calls instead of system calls. Different team members get different answers to the same question, depending on the day, the leader's energy level, or the relationship. This breeds resentment and confusion, not accountability.

Behavior Three: The leader avoids difficult accountability conversations. This is the most common tell. An Operator who was individually excellent often built their reputation on personal performance, not on holding others to standards. The team quickly learns that the stated standard and the enforced standard are different things. These behaviors are not permanent—but they will not correct themselves. The leader must actively choose a different approach.

The Fastest Path Through the Promotion Gap

The first ninety days in a new leadership role define the range of outcomes available for the next two years. Most leaders waste them. Here is the path that shortens the gap.

90-DAY COMMAND INSTALLATION

- Days 1–30: Observe only. Do not change anything. Map the operation as it actually runs.
- Interview every team member: What works? What breaks? What do you wish leadership understood? Read the honest readout before you have a stake in defending it.
- Days 31–60: Design one system based on what you observed. Install it. Communicate why.
- This signals to the team you lead from design, not from reaction.
- Days 61–90: Install one accountability structure. Define the Three-Strike Rule clearly and publicly. Follow through the first time the structure is tested. Consistency in the first 90 days sets the tolerance band for everything after.

Leaders who spend that window performing rather than building rarely recover the lost ground.

> LESSON
>
> *The leaders who stall spend the first 90 days performing competence. The leaders who accelerate spend the first 90 days building command.*

CHAPTER 11

The Hero Trap: Ownership Over Heroics

Chapter 3 established the reward architecture of the Hero Trap: every time you personally save a situation the system should have handled, you get immediate positive feedback—and the system gets weaker. This chapter moves to the solution. Recognizing the pattern is not enough. You have to replace it with something structural.

There is a meaningful distinction between stepping in once and stepping in as a pattern. Stepping in once—when the situation is genuinely extraordinary, when the system is simply not equipped for the event—is competent leadership. It is a bridge. The critical discipline is asking, after that bridge is crossed: what needs to change so we do not need this bridge again? That question is what separates a leader from a hero. The leader uses the rescue as diagnostic data. The hero uses it as proof of their own indispensability.

The word indispensable should create discomfort here. Operations leaders often experience indispensability as a compliment—evidence that they are truly necessary, truly skilled, irreplaceable. The System Commander reads indispensability as an alarm. If the operation cannot function when you are absent for forty-eight hours, you have not built a system. You have built a dependency. And dependencies are fragile by definition. Every rescue the hero performs is a direct investment in fragility. The team's capacity atrophies. When that leader eventually moves on—through promotion, transfer, or departure—what remains is a team that has never been required to function without a hero, now facing a world that will not send them one.

CASE STUDY // THE HERO LEADER

I watched a leader who was, by every surface measure, exceptional. Always moving. Always fixing. Always in the middle of every problem.

From the outside: elite.
From the inside: fragile.

Everything moved because they touched it. Nothing moved when they didn't.

When they were promoted and moved to another location, their old operation dropped within a month.

They had not built a team. They had built a dependency. And when they left, the dependency broke.

Hero leaders are created by systems that reward individual performance over system design. Every time a leader gets praised for personally saving a situation, they are being trained to keep saving situations rather than preventing them.

The organization does not need another hero. It needs an owner for every process—someone who ensures the standard is met whether the leader is there or not.

Breaking the hero pattern requires one decision: stop stepping in as the default. Instead, ask: who owns this? What is the standard? What is the consequence? If those questions do not have answers, that is the real problem to solve.

THE OWNERSHIP RULE

- Every task must have one owner, one standard, and one consequence.
- No shared ownership. No confusion. No excuses.

Shared ownership is no ownership. When everyone is responsible, no one is. Walk your operation and list every critical process. Ask: who owns each one? If the answer is everyone—ownership is not assigned. Fix that.

The shift from hero to owner-builder is not humility. It is strategy. One path leads to indispensability. The other leads to command.

> ***"You are not the solution. You are the architect of the solution. Stop performing and start designing."***

> LESSON
>
> *Ownership is not a burden you give someone. It is a respect you show them—and the highest form of leadership available to you.*

CHAPTER 12

Clarity + Accountability = Control

> ***"Clarity without accountability is ignored. Accountability without clarity is resented. Together—they create control."***

Without clarity, accountability becomes arbitrary—consequences that feel personal rather than structural. Without accountability, clarity becomes aspirational—standards that everyone acknowledges and few actually hold. The combination is what makes a control system real. Both are required. Neither functions alone.

CASE STUDY // INCONSISTENT EXECUTION

Same task. Different result every day.

Root cause: No scoreboard. No clear standard. No check. No consequence.

System fix:

—Visible scoreboard: "Zone recovered: YES / NO by 4:00"

—Defined standard: all facings full, floor clear

—Check: lead verifies at 4:15

—Consequence: miss = immediate recovery + debrief

Result: consistency replaced variability within one week.

LESSON

If it can be interpreted, it will be ignored. Write the standard so clearly that there is nothing to interpret.

Clarity tells people what to do. Accountability tells people what happens if they do not. You need both, and they must be present simultaneously. Remove either one, and the system you have built is not a system—it is a wish dressed in professional language.

Most leaders install only one of the two in practice—usually whichever one feels more natural to their temperament. Leaders who are precise and organized install clarity. Leaders who are results-oriented install accountability. And then they wonder why performance is inconsistent, or why the team feels either lost or anxious. The gap is always the same: clarity without accountability, or accountability without clarity.

When Clarity Exists Without Accountability

Picture an operation with well-documented standards. The expectations are written. The processes are defined. The training materials are thorough. The leader can point to binders, boards, and briefings as evidence that the team knows what is expected. And yet the standards are met inconsistently. Some team members follow the process precisely. Others approximate it. Others ignore it entirely when the leader is not watching. The correction is a conversation—not a consequence. There is no predictable outcome for falling below the standard. So the standard becomes a preference, and preferences are optional.

This breeds cynicism—first in the high performers. The team members who consistently meet the standard begin to notice that the team members who do not face no different outcome. The implicit message is that standards are for the people who choose to follow them. High performers are not sustained by preference. They are sustained by fairness. When clarity exists without accountability, fairness disappears.

When Accountability Exists Without Clarity

Now picture the inverse. The leader runs a tight operation. Consequences are real. Performance is tracked. But the standard itself was never defined precisely. Team members are held accountable to an expectation that was communicated informally, interpreted individually, and never written into a verifiable process. The leader knows what good looks like. The team is guessing.

This breeds fear. Not the productive tension of high standards—actual fear, because the rules are invisible and the consequences are real. Team members spend cognitive energy trying to read the leader's mood rather than executing the process. Accountability applied to unclear expectations is not discipline. It is punishment. And punishment without clarity produces anxiety, concealment, and attrition. The team does not know how to succeed. They only know how to fail.

The Clarity-Accountability Formula in Practice

Pick one critical process in your current operation. Write the standard for that process in one sentence. Not a paragraph—a sentence. If you cannot state it in one sentence, it is not clear enough to be operational. Now assign the accountability structure. Define who owns verification. Define the consequence for a first miss. Define the Three-Strike Rule for that process specifically: what happens at the first deviation, the second, and the third. Write it down.

Now communicate both together—the clarity and the accountability—in the same conversation. Do not introduce the standard in one meeting and the consequence three weeks later when someone misses it. That sequence trains the team to view accountability as a surprise rather than a structure. Present them together, consistently, from day one.

CLARITY + ACCOUNTABILITY CHECKLIST

1. Can I state the standard for this process in one sentence without hesitation?
2. Does every team member responsible know the standard without being prompted?
3. Is there a defined, written consequence for the first deviation from this standard?
4. Has the Three-Strike Rule been communicated explicitly, with all three levels defined?
5. In the last 30 days, has a deviation produced a consequence consistent with what was communicated? If no—your accountability structure is theoretical.

> LESSON
>
> *Clarity without accountability is instruction. Accountability without clarity is pressure. Neither produces control. A System Commander installs both simultaneously, measures the output, and adjusts the design—not the people—when the output falls short.*

CHAPTER 13

Accountability at Scale

Accountability is not a conversation. It is not a reminder. It is not a coaching session. Accountability is the only currency that produces lasting behavior change. And the test is simple: if behavior does not change, something called accountability happened—but real accountability did not.

The dominant model of accountability is a conversation. One person does something wrong. The leader addresses it directly, makes the expectation clear, and the exchange constitutes accountability. In small operations with small teams, this model can function.

But it has a structural ceiling. It can only reach as far as the leader's energy, attention, and willingness to confront on any given day.

In a large-scale operation—dozens of employees, multiple departments, multiple shifts—accountability cannot be a conversation the leader chooses to have when they have bandwidth. It becomes inconsistent. And when accountability is inconsistent, the team learns something precise: the standard is not really the standard. The standard is whatever the leader decides to enforce today. That is not a standard. That is a mood.

When the team figures out that accountability is mood-dependent, behavior adjusts accordingly. They watch the leader's energy level. They learn which days they can get away with it and which days they cannot. Enforcement becomes an obstacle they navigate around rather than a structure they operate within. This is not a team failure. It is an architecture failure. The accountability system was built on a single point—the leader's daily willingness to confront—and single points of failure always fail.

The System Commander thinks about accountability differently. Not as a conversation that happens after a problem is identified, but as a mechanism built into the architecture so that problems surface automatically, consequences attach predictably, and the leader's personal energy is not the variable that determines whether any of it happens. This is what accountability at scale actually means: the system itself becomes confrontational, so the leader does not have to be confrontational in isolation every day.

Structural accountability looks like this: standards are posted and specific, not verbal and vague. Checkpoints are built into the shift at scheduled intervals, not triggered by the leader's mood to inspect. Documentation exists so that a pattern of behavior is visible over time, not dependent on the leader's memory of past conversations. Consequences are known in advance—not invented at the moment of confrontation—so they land as the predictable result of a known rule rather than the personal reaction of an irritated manager. When all of those elements exist, the system holds the accountability and the leader reinforces it. That is a fundamentally different posture than a leader carrying the entire weight of enforcement on their own shoulders. The goal is not to make the leader more confrontational. The goal is to make the confrontation structural.

CASE STUDY // THE WALK-BY LEADER

Leader sees a miss. Internal response: "I'll address that later."
Walks away.
What the team observes: "They saw it and kept walking."
What the team concludes: "It doesn't matter."
Standard drops. Next week, the floor is worse. And the leader is surprised.

LAW—ACCOUNTABILITY LAW

"Delayed accountability is no accountability. Address the miss now—or accept it as the new standard."

> LESSON
>
> *The immediate-response framework from Chapter 8 applies here at scale: direct, immediate, and documented. The difference at scale is that the mechanism triggering the response must be structural—not dependent on you spotting the miss personally. You cannot build accountability in a conference room. You build it on the floor, in the moment, every time.*

PART III—REFLECTION QUESTIONS

Scale: Ownership, Accountability, and Command

Part III confronts what happens when you try to grow without transferring true ownership. Promotion without preparation and heroics without systems are not signs of a strong leader—they are signs of an operation that will collapse the moment you remove yourself.

1. Think about the last person you promoted from your team. What specific system did you install to prepare them before the promotion happened? If the answer is "I gave them more responsibility to see how they handled it," that is not development—that is audition without training.

2. Are you the hero in your operation? When a crisis hits, does your team come to you first because the system points to you, or because no one else has been built to handle it? Name the last crisis that was resolved without your direct involvement. If you cannot, you are the hero. That is a problem.

3. Describe the current accountability structure in your operation. When a standard is missed, what happens, by whom, within what timeframe, and with what documented consequence? If you cannot answer all four parts of that question, you do not have an accountability structure.

4. Have you applied the Three-Strike Rule consistently in the last six months? Name a situation where someone missed the same standard three or more times. Did you execute the Three-Strike Rule? If not, name the exact reason—and then assess whether that reason was operational or personal.

5. What would your team's performance look like in month two if you were completely removed from the operation? Month two—after the initial scramble. Would it hold, decline slowly, or fall apart?

6. Identify the person on your team who is most capable of replacing you. What is the specific gap between where they are today and where they need to be? What have you done in the last 30 days to close that gap?

7. Where in your operation does accountability stop because of someone's tenure or relationship with you? Name the person and the standard they are not being held to. Seniority is not immunity.

8. What is the difference between clarity and assumption in your operation right now? Pick your lowest-performing team member. Can they state their three most critical responsibilities and the exact standard for each—without you prompting them?

CLOSING CHALLENGE—PART III

- If the performance of your operation depends on your personal presence, you have not built command—you have built dependency.
- Your job is to make yourself operationally unnecessary at the level below you, so you can command at the level above you. Start that transfer today.

PART IV

Execute: Living as a System Commander

CHAPTER 14

The Real Job of a Leader

The common assumption about leadership is that it is about managing people. It is not.

> ***"Your job is to solve problems at speed. If you're not solving problems faster than they arrive, you are losing control."***

That shift—from managing people to solving problems—makes leadership concrete and measurable.

THE PROBLEM-SOLVING HIERARCHY

1. Immediate: Anything actively costing performance right now.
2. Structural: Recurring problems that need a system fix.
3. Developmental: Problems requiring coaching over time.

- Most leaders focus on Developmental while Immediate and Structural go unaddressed.
- System Commanders invert this. They stabilize and develop within a stable system.

This misunderstanding is nearly universal. A new manager walks onto the floor believing their primary function is to develop people—to coach, to inspire, to cultivate culture. That instinct sounds right. But when you apply it to a floor that is operationally broken, development becomes a form of avoidance. You are having a performance conversation inside a building where the system never gave that person a fair shot at performing correctly.

The problem-solving hierarchy exists because not all problems are the same kind, yet most leaders treat them as if they are. An Immediate problem is a break in function right now—a process not running, a standard being violated, an operation bleeding today. A Structural problem is the architecture underneath that break—the unclear expectation, the unowned responsibility, the process that was never written down correctly. A Developmental problem is a gap in a person—their skill, their judgment, their consistency. These three tiers require different interventions, different urgency, and different amounts of your time.

Here is the failure pattern in most operations: leaders invert the hierarchy. They spend the majority of their attention at the Developmental level because that is where human interaction lives, and most people—even serious, hard-working managers—are more comfortable in conversation than in system design. Coaching feels productive. It generates goodwill. Meanwhile, the Structural layer sits with undefined ownership and misaligned processes, and the Immediate layer breaks something new every morning. You cannot coach your way out of a structural problem. Telling someone to perform better inside a system that makes performing correctly nearly impossible is not development. It is blame wearing a mentorship costume.

The sequence is non-negotiable. Immediate problems must be addressed first because they are happening now and costing you now. You do not sit down for a developmental conversation while a process is actively failing. Stop the bleeding first. Once the floor is stable, you go to the Structural level. You ask why the break happened. You find the gap in the system. You close it. Only then does a developmental conversation have real meaning—because at that point, you are addressing a genuine gap in a person operating inside a functional structure. Everything before that point is noise.

You can identify a leader who is prioritizing correctly by watching the decisions they make under pressure. When a process breaks, the wrong leader schedules a team meeting. The right leader fixes the process today, builds a check to ensure it does not break again tomorrow, then addresses whether a person needs additional support. When a standard is ignored, the wrong leader says the team needs better culture. The right leader identifies who owns that standard, confirms the consequence was never applied, and closes that loop before the end of the shift. The first question when something goes wrong is not "Who needs coaching?" It is: "What broke, and what in the system allowed it?"

> LESSON
>
> *Your value is not your title. It is your ability to solve problems under pressure.*

A leader operating at the wrong tier has a recognizable time signature. The calendar shows back-to-back one-on-ones. The week is full of coaching conversations, performance discussions, and check-ins. Frequent team huddles are scheduled. On paper, this looks like engaged leadership. In practice, it is a symptom. Alongside all that conversation, the operation continues producing recurring fires—the same categories of problems surfacing week after week, handled, resolved, and then reappearing. If a leader spends the majority of available time in developmental mode while the operation continues generating immediate and structural problems, the problem-solving sequence has been inverted. The coaching sessions are not fixing the operation because the operation does not have a coaching problem.

The inversion is not usually conscious. It is comfort-driven. Coaching conversations have a visible structure, a clear beginning and end, and a human on the other side who can nod and engage. Structural problem-solving—redesigning a check, rewriting a process, installing a new accountability loop—is harder to schedule, harder to evaluate, and slower to show results. Leaders drift toward what feels productive and measurable, and coaching feels both. That is the trap. A leader who is comfortable in developmental mode will stay there even when the operation demands work at a different tier.

A leader operating at the right tier has a different time signature entirely. They spend the majority of time in the operation, not in scheduled conversations. They catch problems at the Immediate tier before those problems require a Developmental conversation. The checks built into the system flag deviations early enough that a brief, direct correction handles them—no sit-down meeting required. When developmental work is appropriate, it is time-bounded and tied to a specific system gap the person needs to close. The result is an operation that generates fewer crises over time because problems are intercepted by the architecture before they escalate into the kind of issue that requires a leader's personal intervention.

CHAPTER 15

The System Commander Daily Audit

Identity is not maintained through inspiration alone. It is maintained through daily practice. The System Commander Daily Audit is a five-question self-check done at the end of every shift. It takes less than five minutes. When practiced consistently, its impact compounds.

THE SYSTEM COMMANDER DAILY AUDIT

1. Did I enforce at least one standard today? Immediately and without negotiation?
YES / NO

2. Did I address any miss by changing the system? Or did I repeat myself and move on?
YES / NO

3. Did I perform work today that belongs to the system, not to me?
YES / NO

4. Did at least one team member solve a problem today without bringing it to me?
YES / NO

5. If I had not been here today, what specifically would have broken—and why?
YES / NO

Score:
One point per honest yes.
Three consecutive days below 3: Rebuild, don't motivate.

The Five Questions in Detail

This audit is not a reflection exercise. It is a diagnostic—five specific questions designed to catch the exact failure modes that erode System Commander leadership over time: deferred enforcement, repeated corrections, personal substitution for system function, team dependency, and unclosed operational exposure.

Answer each question honestly. A comfortable answer that is not true is not an answer. It is avoidance at the end of a long day, and it costs you tomorrow.

Question 1: Did I enforce at least one standard today?

Coaching note: If the answer is no, the standard existed only on paper today. Find the specific moment—and there was one—when you saw a miss and let it go. Maybe it was the wrong time. Maybe the team member was already stressed. Maybe you told yourself you would circle back. That moment is your starting point tomorrow. The question is not whether problems occurred. Problems always occur. The question is whether your enforcement was real. Real enforcement is specific, immediate, and consistent. If it did not happen today, note the exact situation so you can address it when it comes back. It will come back.

Question 2: Did I address any miss by changing the system?

Coaching note: Repetition is the signal. If you said the same thing this week that you said last week—to the same person, about the same behavior, in the same situation—you addressed a symptom. You did not address the system. If you changed a process, wrote a standard, assigned an owner, defined a consequence, or removed a step that was creating the failure, you addressed the system. Count how many times today you repeated yourself. That number is your system-building backlog. If the number is three, you have three systems to build. Prioritize the one you have repeated most often—repetition frequency is a direct measure of how long a system gap has been ignored.

Question 3: Did I perform work that belongs to the system?

Coaching note: List specifically what you did with your own hands today that a well-designed system should have handled. Not generally—specifically. The coverage call you made because there was no coverage protocol. The signage correction you made personally because no one had been assigned ownership. The count you ran because the verification process was never defined. Every item on that list is a system you have not built yet. This is not about guilt—it is inventory. You cannot build what you have not named. Write the list. The items that appear on it most often across multiple days are your highest-priority builds. Start there.

Question 4: Did my team solve a problem without me?

Coaching note: If the answer is yes, note what type of problem it was and what gave that team member the authority or clarity to resolve it. That is a replicable system. If the answer is no—and if it has been no for three days in a row—your team is dependent. Dependency is not their failure. It is a system design problem. Ask one specific question: what does the team member who brought you the last problem need—defined authority, a documented process, a clear escalation threshold—to resolve that category of problem without you next time? The answer to that question is the system you need to build. Not a conversation. Not a reminder. A structure that makes the decision available without requiring your presence.

Question 5: What would have broken if I hadn't been here?

Coaching note: This is the core accountability question. Answer it specifically. Not "things would have been chaotic"—name what specifically would have failed and the exact reason. This is the Test 3 question applied daily. Over time, the answer to this question should get shorter. The list of things that only work because you were there should shrink as you build the systems that replace your personal presence. If the answer is getting longer—if more things depend on you this month than last month—you are not building. You are accumulating. Every item on this list is a system you need to build. If the list is long, do not try to build all of it at once. Start with the answer that appears most often. That is the highest-leverage build in your operation right now.

The Scoring System

Each question is scored 0 or 1. Score 1 if your answer was yes and you can support it with a specific, concrete example. Score 0 if the answer was no, if the answer was vague, or if you cannot name a specific situation that confirms it.

A score of 5 means every question produced a yes backed by a real example. It means enforcement happened, system-building happened, the team demonstrated independence, and your personal operational exposure is documented and being addressed. This is the target.

A score of 3 or below on three consecutive days means you are operating in reactive leadership mode. You are enforcing inconsistently, repeating corrections instead of building fixes, performing work the system should handle, and carrying exposure that is not shrinking. When this pattern appears, do not try to course-correct at the daily audit level. Go back to Phase 1 of the 30-Day Plan. Identify which of the five failure modes is driving the score, and treat it as a system gap—not a motivation problem. That is what it is.

The audit is not a performance review. It exists to catch drift before drift becomes the new standard. Five minutes at the end of a shift is a fraction of what it costs to rebuild a team that has learned the system will not hold.

> LESSON
>
> *Daily practice builds permanent identity. The audit is not a report card. It is a mirror.*

It works because of what it does to your behavior before the shift ends. When you know you will be scoring yourself on five honest questions at the end of the day, you start making different decisions at ten in the morning. You see a standard being violated at 9:45 and you think: if I walk past this, I already know what my score looks like tonight. That is not guilt—that is accountability operating the way it should. The audit makes the abstract concrete. Leadership—which has no single metric, no daily output number, no visible scoreboard—suddenly has five data points attached to it. You either enforced today, or you did not. You either prevented recurrence, or you did not. There is no comfortable middle ground to hide in.

This is why the audit is not a reporting tool. It is a behavioral governor. A reporting tool tells someone else what happened. A behavioral governor changes what you do while there is still time to act differently. Most operations leaders go home at the end of a shift knowing whether the numbers hit. What they almost never sit with honestly is whether they actually led that day. Whether they enforced a standard they had been avoiding. Whether they identified a recurring problem and closed the structural gap underneath it, or just addressed the surface symptom again. Numbers tell you what the operation produced. The audit tells you what you built.

The pattern of scores over ninety days is the real data. A single low score on any question is noise. A consistent pattern is a diagnosis. A leader who scores low repeatedly on "Did I enforce today?" has an avoidance pattern—choosing comfort over command, letting violations accumulate because confrontation feels costly in the moment. A leader who consistently scores low on "Did I prevent recurrence?" is stuck in Operator mode—handling the same break, shift after shift, without ever going to the Structural level to close the root cause. The audit does not produce these diagnoses on its own. The leader has to be honest enough to read the pattern and name it accurately. That honesty is part of the discipline.

Ninety days of audit scores is a leadership profile. It shows you where your floor is. It shows you which failure modes—unclear standards, unowned processes, unenforced consequences—you are tolerating most. No external evaluation will show you this as clearly, because no external observer sees every decision you made or avoided during the shift. You do. The audit is the mechanism that forces you to turn that knowledge into data, and data into change.

CHAPTER 16

The Identity Test

Knowing the system is not the test. Operating as a System Commander when conditions are hard is the test.

Passing Test 1 when conditions are easy is not the measure. System Commanders are defined by what they do when conditions are hard. The system does not have feelings. The system does not have bad days. The standard is the standard regardless of circumstance.

THE IDENTITY TEST

1. Test 1: You see a miss at the end of a 12-hour shift. Do you address it now—or tell yourself you'll catch it tomorrow?
2. Test 2: A standard breaks three shifts in a row. Do you repeat the expectation—or redesign the system?
3. Test 3: Your operation runs perfectly when you're there. Does it hold the same standard when you're not? (see Chapter 16)

Test 1 gets passed some of the time. Fewer leaders pass Test 2. Almost no one passes Test 3 without deliberately building toward it.

Test 3 is the entire point of this book.

Passing Test 3 is a structural achievement, not a personal one. It cannot be willed into existence through a renewed commitment to high standards or sharper in-the-moment accountability. Leaders who believe their operation will hold without them because they care more or communicate better are working from the wrong model. The operation that runs without the leader runs because three structural conditions are simultaneously in place. Without all three, the leader's absence is a countdown.

The first condition is a documented standard system specific enough to be executable without interpretation. Not a values statement—a written standard that defines what done looks like, who is responsible, how it is verified, and at what frequency. The test is simple: could a competent person, new to this operation, execute and verify the standard correctly using only what is written? If no, the standard is not documented. It is stored, and stored standards do not hold when the person they are stored in leaves the building.

The second condition is a self-reinforcing consequence structure in which missed standards produce a defined outcome independently—not because the leader happened to be watching and chose to act. The consequence does not have to be disciplinary. It can be a re-do requirement, a check-in trigger, or an escalation. What it must be is pre-defined, known to the team in advance, and applied consistently without the leader's daily judgment as the activation mechanism. When consequence requires the leader to decide whether to apply it, the structure is leader-dependent—which is Test 3's failure mode.

The third condition is the hardest to build and the most commonly absent: secondary leaders who carry the culture, not just execute the tasks. The operation that holds without the leader holds because someone present is making decisions consistent with the standard, applying the consequence structure, and modeling the expectation under pressure. That person is not made in a week. They are developed through deliberate coaching, progressively expanded responsibility, and the leader's willingness to let them handle situations independently. Most operations have secondary leaders who can run the day. Fewer have secondary leaders who will defend the standard when it costs something.

That gap—between a leader's self-image and the operation's actual record—has a name. Most leaders, if asked honestly, would describe themselves as consistent, fair, and high-standard. They have evidence for this—specific moments, specific decisions. What they often cannot see is the pattern between those moments: standards applied inconsistently, consequences defined but not followed, team members who have learned precisely how much the standard flexes. The operation's record does not weigh intentions. Closing the gap begins with accepting that record as the honest score.

The irreversibility point is the target of this entire book. Before reaching it, the System Commander identity requires deliberate reinforcement at every pressure point. After reaching it, the identity shapes instinct rather than decision-making alone. The leader still makes choices, but the default has shifted. The operation's health becomes something the leader is constitutionally unwilling to allow to degrade, and the system reflects that intolerance structurally rather than personally. Getting to that point is the work. Every component in this book is load-bearing.

> LAW—THE IDENTITY LAW
>
> *"You are not the leader you think you are. You are the leader your operation reflects. Look at what holds without you. That is your real score. The question is not who you want to be—it is what your operation reveals about who you already are."*

> LESSON
>
> *Identity is not declared. It is demonstrated. The floor under pressure is the only test that counts.*

CHAPTER 17

Command in Any Operation

The System Commander framework works in any environment where standards must hold and leaders must perform without constant supervision. Whether you are running a restaurant, a distribution center, a hospital department, a corporate team, or a retail operation, the specific standards differ. The tools are the same.

Why does the framework transfer? Because the failure modes transfer. The specific variables change with the environment—the product, the pace, the regulatory environment, the staffing model. But the way operations break down is not specific to any of those environments. Operations collapse in three ways, every time, in every industry: the standard was unclear, the process had no single owner, or the consequence never arrived. These are not retail problems. They are human organizational problems, and they appear anywhere people are responsible for consistent output under changing conditions.

This is why the tools built to address those failure modes work across contexts. A Standard-Check-Consequence loop does not care whether the standard is about food temperature, inventory accuracy, discharge timing, or order fulfillment. The mechanism is identical: define what correct looks like, verify that it is happening, and respond when it is not. An Ownership Rule does not care whether the process being owned involves stocking shelves, routing packages, or processing insurance claims. It cares that one person is responsible, that they know it, and that the accountability is real. The framework is not a retail system that happens to resemble something useful elsewhere. It is a structural solution to a structural problem that shows up everywhere human beings run operations together.

The objection is predictable: "my operation is different." Every leader believes this. And they are not entirely wrong—the complexity does vary. A trauma unit operates at a different pace than a retail stockroom. But complexity is not the issue. The structural failure modes are not complex problems—they are simple problems that have been allowed to persist. A hospital department with unclear standards around documentation is not failing because medicine is complicated. It is failing for the same reason a retail floor with unclear standards around zone recovery fails: no one defined what correct looks like with enough precision to hold anyone to it. The specific content of the standard changes. The failure mode of not having one does not.

The "my operation is different" objection is almost always a defense against the accountability that comes with a clear system. If the framework does not apply here, then you cannot be measured against it. The variables that genuinely make operations different—industry, scale, regulatory constraints, staffing ratios—affect the content of your standards. They do not affect the need for standards, the need for ownership, or the need for consequences. Those three requirements are not retail preferences. They are operational physics.

THE COMMAND STARTER—5 STEPS

- **Step 1: Name the five biggest recurring problems.**
(What fails every week, without fail?)
- **Step 2: For each—define the standard.**
(Done or not done. Binary.)
- **Step 3: Assign one owner.**
(One name. No shared responsibility.)
- **Step 4: Install the check.**
(When will it be verified? Before the deadline.)
- **Step 5: Define and apply the consequence.**
(What happens at the moment of a miss?)

Do this for five problems. In two weeks, repeat for five more. In three months, your operation will look entirely different—not because you worked harder, but because you built control.

> LESSON
>
> *Control scales. Effort does not. Build control first, and scale from there.*

CHAPTER 18

Building a Bench of System Commanders

> ***"The goal is not to be the only System Commander. The goal is to build more of them."***

The Bench Builder

The original version of this methodology fit on a Post-it note. Three bullets. The idea was right. The execution guide was not there. What follows is the full methodology—not theory, not framework language, but the actual sequence of decisions and actions that turns a high performer into a System Commander.

Section 1: Who to Choose

Talent identification is the first place this fails. Most leaders promote the person who works hardest, complains least, and executes without being managed. That person is valuable. They are not necessarily the person you need for this.

There are three behavioral tells that separate a future System Commander from a high performer who will remain an Operator.

First: they notice when a process is broken, not just when a task is left undone. Ask them what went wrong on a bad shift and listen to how they describe it. An Operator says someone did not do their job. A future System Commander says the system did not catch it—and then describes which part of the system failed and why it was set up to fail. They are already diagnosing at the level you need them to lead.

Second: they get frustrated by recurring problems—not just tired of them. Fatigue is passive. Frustration at recurrence is active. It means they are keeping score. They remember that this broke last Tuesday and the Tuesday before. That memory, combined with the frustration, is a diagnostic instinct. It is the beginning of a system thinker.

Third: when given expanded responsibility, they ask "What is the standard?" before they ask "What do I do?" They want the architecture before the instructions. They understand, even if they cannot articulate it yet, that execution without a standard is merely motion.

The contrast matters. A high performer without these tells will execute brilliantly within a defined scope and struggle the moment ownership is genuine. They will wait to be told. They will manage the task but not the system. Promoting them into system ownership without these tells is not a development move—it is the promotion problem repeating itself at the next level. You have not built a bench. You have moved a high performer into a role they will not thrive in and created a gap where you thought you had a solution.

Section 2: The First Assignment

Give them one system to own completely. Not a project. Not an initiative. Not a task with an end date. A system: one written standard, one scheduled check, one defined consequence. Their name on the result.

The reason it is one—not two, not three—is that ownership at scale begins with ownership of one. A leader who has never fully owned a system does not yet understand what ownership costs. They have not felt the weight of a standard they wrote being held against results they produced. They have not had to apply a consequence to someone they work alongside every day. They have not run a check that found a failure they are now responsible for fixing. The first assignment is where they learn all of that.

It also surfaces the failure modes early, when they are still correctable. Most newly developing System Commanders will write a standard that is too vague—language that sounds accountable but gives everyone an exit. They will run a check that is too infrequent—weekly when it needs to be daily, informal when it needs to be documented. They will hesitate on the first consequence. Every one of these is expected. Every one of these is a coaching opportunity, not a disqualifier. The two-week side-by-side period exists precisely to catch these failures before they harden into habits.

Do not simplify the first assignment to protect them from the difficulty. The difficulty is the point.

Section 3: The Two-Week Coaching Protocol

This is not shadowing. It is not mentorship. It is not observation. It is structured transfer—a deliberate, sequenced handoff of system ownership that follows a specific protocol.

Week 1: The leader runs the system. The developing System Commander watches, asks questions, and begins to understand what running the system actually requires—not in the abstract, but in real time, with real conditions and real failures. At the end of each shift, the leader runs a three-question debrief: What held? What broke? What would you do differently? The third question is not rhetorical. It is the beginning of the developing leader's diagnostic voice. Push for specificity. "I would do it differently" is not an answer. "The check needs to happen at 7 AM instead of 9 because the correction window closes before 8" is an answer.

Week 2: The developing System Commander runs the system. The leader observes. The leader does not intervene to correct technique, smooth a rough interaction, or pre-empt a minor failure. The only intervention is when a consequence is being avoided—when the developing leader is clearly deciding not to apply it. That intervention is not a rescue. It is a direct conversation, on the floor, in the moment: "You saw what I saw. What is the consequence? Apply it." Then step back and let them.

The debrief in Week 2 uses the same three questions. The answers should start shifting. By the end of Week 2, a developing System Commander who is ready will begin identifying their own failure modes before you name them.

The handoff moment is a specific conversation, not a general transition. At the end of Week 2, the leader sits down with the developing System Commander and says: "This system is yours. I will inspect it, not run it. If a standard breaks, your name is on the fix. If the consequence isn't applied, we have a conversation. I am not taking it back." That last sentence is not a threat. It is a commitment—to them, and to the integrity of the development process.

After the handoff, the leader inspects the output, not the process. Walk the result. Did the standard hold? Was the check documented? Was the consequence applied when it needed to be? Inspect once per shift for the first 30 days. Not to hover—to close the loop. The developing System Commander needs to know the inspection is real.

Section 4: When It Fails

It will fail. Expect it. Something will break—a consequence gets skipped because the day was hard, a standard gets quietly rewritten to be easier to hit, a check migrates from documented to informal because informal is faster. None of these is a reason to pull back the assignment.

When failure happens, the leader's job is to identify which of the three components broke—the standard, the check, or the consequence—and rebuild that component with the developing System Commander, not for them. The distinction matters. Rebuilding it for them teaches dependence. Rebuilding it with them teaches diagnosis. The goal is a System Commander who, the next time their system breaks, identifies the failure mode themselves and brings you the corrected component. That is the irreversibility point. When they can diagnose their own system, the bench has one name on it.

Do this three times, with three different people. You have a bench. Do it across your organization. You have a culture—not a culture you declared, but one you built, consequence by consequence, check by check, one system at a time.

> LESSON
>
> *The goal is not to be the best operator in the room. It is to build a room full of operators who no longer need you to be.*

PART IV—REFLECTION QUESTIONS

Execute: Living as a System Commander

Part IV is where theory ends and daily discipline begins. Knowing what a System Commander is and actually living as one are separated by the choices you make before 9 AM every morning. This section demands that you audit your daily behavior against your stated identity and tell the truth about what you find.

1. Describe your daily audit process. Not aspirationally—what you actually do, in what sequence, at what time, every single day. If you do not have a documented daily audit, you are not commanding your operation—you are touring it.

2. Think about the last time a standard was missed in your operation and you found out about it later—not in real time. What does that delay tell you about your visibility system?

3. What is your real job as a leader right now? Not your job description—your actual highest-leverage activity. Are you spending the majority of your time doing that, or are you doing work that belongs to the level below you?

4. Identify the moment in the last two weeks when you compromised a standard because you were tired, distracted, or under pressure. What did that moment cost you in credibility and team culture?

5. An identity test: when conditions are hard—high volume, short-staffed, under scrutiny—does your behavior as a leader improve, stay the same, or degrade? What does your team see from you when the operation is under the most pressure?

6. Who on your bench is 60 days from being ready to step up and take meaningful ownership of a system? If the answer is no one, what does that say about how you have been spending your development time?

7. What is the one behavior you exhibit that your team is most likely to model—for better or worse? What would it cost your operation if every person on your team adopted it at full scale?

8. Where in your daily behavior is there a visible gap between the standard you hold your team to and the standard you hold yourself to? Your team sees it. Name it.

CLOSING CHALLENGE—PART IV

- Execution is not a phase—it is the permanent state of a System Commander.
- You do not get to finish installing the system and then coast.
- Every day is an audit. Every day is an identity test.
- Every day you either command your operation or you let it command you.

PART V

Transform: Your First 30 Days

V

CHAPTER 19

Your First 30 Days as a System Commander

The work begins when the reading ends. Most leadership books close with inspiration and a vague call to action. This one closes with a plan—a specific, structured guide for the first 30 days of operating as a System Commander. Do not skip this chapter.

BEFORE YOU BEGIN

- Complete the Control System Readiness Assessment in Appendix A before starting Day 1.
- Your score establishes your baseline. You will retake it at Day 30.
- The gap between your two scores is your measure of progress.

The five questions below are not rhetorical. They are the diagnostic that determines where Phase 1 starts. Answer them in writing before Day 1.

1. What are the five most costly recurring failures in my operation right now? Not the loudest—the most expensive in time lost, labor wasted, or downstream rework.

2. Of those five failures, how many have a written standard currently assigned to them? If the answer is zero, you don't just have an accountability problem—you have a standards problem. Start there.

3. Of those five failures, how many have a single named owner—one person, not a team or a role?

4. Of those five failures, how many have a documented consequence that has been applied consistently in the last 30 days?

5. If you were removed from your operation for 30 days starting tomorrow, what would break first—and why? Be specific. Name the process, name the gap, name the person who would be in over their head.

Write the answers down. You will return to these exact five questions on Day 28. The gap between your answers today and your answers then is the measure of everything this plan is designed to build.

Phase 1—Days 1–10: Define and Assign

The first ten days have one purpose: build the minimum viable system. Not a complete system. Not a perfect system. Five standards, five owners, five checks. That is the output. Everything else in this phase is the work required to produce that output.

Days 1–3: Standard Identification

Walk the operation with your baseline questions in hand. Do not fix anything. Do not comment on anything. Do not pull anyone aside to redirect them. You are mapping, not managing. This distinction matters: the moment you start correcting things before you have standards written, you establish yourself as a leader who manages by reaction. That is not the system.

As you walk, write down every recurring problem you observe or already know exists. Do not filter the list yet. Get it on paper. Most operations have fifteen to twenty recurring failures that anyone with two weeks of experience could name. Write them all down.

Then filter. From that full list, select the five problems that cost the most performance every week. Not the most visible. Not the ones that generate the most complaints. The most costly—in time lost, labor wasted, customer impact, or downstream rework. The loudest problem in any operation is rarely the most expensive one. The missed freight deadline that creates a three-hour recovery every morning costs more than the employee who parks in the wrong spot. Focus on cost.

Write each standard using the four-component format from Chapter 5: specific observable behavior, one named owner, a specific deadline, and a verification method.

What this looks like in practice: A common problem in large retail operations is freight that is not finished before the location opens to customers. The vague version of this standard is: "Freight should be done before we open." That is not a standard. It has no owner, no specific deadline, and no verification method. A written standard using the four-component format looks like this:

STANDARD: All freight from the overnight delivery is processed, stocked, and back-stock staged in the receiving area with trash removed by 6:45 AM. Owner: Marcus T. Deadline: 6:45 AM daily. Verification: Manager walk of all affected departments by 6:50 AM, confirmed in the shift log.

That is a standard. You can enforce it, check it, and hand it off. "Freight should be done before we open" is a hope. Know the difference.

By the end of Day 3, you have five standards written on paper. That is the only acceptable output for this period.

Days 4–6: Ownership Assignment

Take your five written standards and assign one owner to each. If you are tempted to assign two owners to a single standard—to cover your bases, to create redundancy, to share accountability—do not. One standard, one owner. Shared ownership is no ownership. When it fails, both owners will point at each other and both will be right.

For each assignment, have a direct face-to-face conversation with that person. Not a group meeting where you announce new expectations to the team. Not a text. Not an email. A one-on-one conversation, in person, where you hand them the written standard and say:

"This is the standard. Here is exactly what done looks like. Here is the deadline. Here is how I will verify it. Your name is on this."

Say those words, or words close to them. The specificity of the language is deliberate. "Your name is on this" communicates ownership without ambiguity. It also communicates that verification will happen—not as a threat, but as a stated fact.

What if they push back?

There are two types of pushback, and they require two different responses.

PUSHBACK TYPE 1 — OPERATIONAL

- "I can't hit 6:45 AM because the delivery truck arrives at 6:15 and we don't have enough people on before 6:30." This is legitimate information. It means the standard needs to be adjusted, or a resource constraint needs to be addressed before the deadline holds. Take this seriously. Revise the standard, solve the constraint, or set an interim deadline while you address the underlying issue. Document the conversation.

PUSHBACK TYPE 2 — MOTIVATIONAL

- "That's not how we've always done it" or "The last manager didn't care about that." This is not information about the standard. This is a test of whether you are serious. Your response is brief and non-reactive: "I understand that. This is how it works now. I'll verify it on [day and time]." Then stop talking. Do not argue. Do not explain the history. Move on.

Document each ownership assignment in writing. A shared notebook, a printed log, a simple spreadsheet—the format does not matter. What matters is that you have a record that shows: the standard, the owner, the date of the conversation, and the first scheduled verification. This documentation is not bureaucracy. It is the foundation of every accountability conversation you will have in Phase 2.

By the end of Day 6, you have five written standards and five named owners. Every owner has received their standard in a direct conversation. Every assignment is documented.

Days 7–10: Check Installation

A standard without a scheduled check is a wish. The check is what separates a written standard from a functioning system. For each of your five standards, install a pre-deadline check: a specific time, on the calendar, before the deadline arrives, at which you verify progress.

This check is not a gut feeling. It is not a casual glance when you happen to be nearby. It is a scheduled moment with a specific purpose.

The check answers three questions, in order:

1. Is the standard on track to be met by the deadline?
2. If not, what is the specific constraint?
3. What needs to happen in the next [X time] to hit the deadline?

The check is not a progress report. Think of it as a decision point. If the standard is on track, you confirm it and move on. If it is not on track, you identify the constraint and make a decision—either remove the constraint or adjust the timeline and hold the owner accountable for the miss. Do not wait until the deadline to discover the standard failed. The check exists precisely to prevent that.

Install the check at the right interval. If the deadline is the end of a shift, the check should happen at the midpoint of the shift. If the deadline is daily, the check should happen at a point early enough that a recovery is still possible. Schedule it on your calendar. Block the time.

By Day 10, you have built the minimum viable system:

MINIMUM VIABLE SYSTEM—DAY 10

5 written standards | Four-component format, on paper

5 named owners | One name per standard

5 scheduled checks | Calendar times, before deadlines

That is Phase 1 complete. You have not fixed the operation. You have installed the structure that allows it to be fixed and held.

Phase 2—Days 11-20: Enforce and Document

The minimum viable system is now installed. Phase 2 determines whether it is real. The difference between a system that exists on paper and a system that governs behavior is enforcement. This phase is where most newly promoted managers fail—not because they do not know what to do, but because they hesitate at the moment it counts.

Days 11–13: First Enforcement

At some point in this stretch, you will see a standard missed. This is not a setback. It is a test—and more importantly, it is an opportunity to define the operation's understanding of what your standards mean.

What you do in the next fifteen minutes after that miss defines the next ninety days.

The System Commander response to a first miss is immediate, direct, and without emotion. You do not wait to have more information. You do not wait until the shift ends. You do not schedule a conversation for later in the week. You walk to the owner and say:

"This is the standard. It is missed right now. Here is what needs to happen in the next [X time]."

Then you verify that it happened.

No lecture. No reference to how serious this is. No motivational framing. The correction is brief because the standard was clear. If the standard was clear, the deadline was clear, and the check was scheduled, there is no need for a long conversation about what went wrong. State the miss, state the correction, verify the outcome.

What you cannot do:

> Wait until you have more information. You have the information. The standard was missed.

> Wait until end of shift. Addressing a miss hours after it happened sends the signal that deadlines are approximate.

> Handle it where no one can see. This does not mean you humiliate anyone publicly. But if the miss happened in a visible area and your response is completely invisible, the team registers: they saw it and said nothing. That signal is permanent.

Document the miss immediately after the correction. Date, standard name, owner's name, what happened, how you responded, and the outcome. This entry is not punitive. It is the data your Phase 2 pattern analysis depends on.

Days 14–17: Pattern Identification

By Day 14, you have enough documented data to see patterns. Pull your log and run this diagnostic on each of your five standards.

For each standard, answer three questions:

1. Has this standard been met consistently?
2. Has it been missed more than once?
3. When it was missed, what was the stated reason?

Then use the three-question diagnostic to identify the root cause of any repeating miss:

Diagnostic Question 1: Is the standard clear enough?

A standard that is missed repeatedly by different people, or by the same person for different stated reasons, is often a clarity problem. The behavior is not observable enough. The deadline has ambiguity. The verification method is undefined. If this is the problem, rewrite the standard using tighter language. Do not blame the owner for a standard that was written to fail.

Diagnostic Question 2: Is the check happening?

A standard that is missed at the deadline but was never checked before the deadline is a check problem. The pre-deadline check either is not happening or is happening too late to allow recovery. If this is the problem, reinstall the check at an earlier point in the timeline. Adjust the calendar entry. Treat it as a structural fix, not a personal failing.

Diagnostic Question 3: Is the consequence real?

A standard that is missed repeatedly despite a clear written expectation and a functioning check is a consequence problem. The owner has learned—through direct experience—that the miss costs less than the effort required to hit the standard. If this is the problem, the consequence needs to be defined explicitly and applied the next time. Not threatened. Applied. Until the consequence is real, the standard is optional. You cannot enforce a standard without a defined outcome for missing it.

Document your pattern analysis. By Day 17, you know which standards are holding, which are fragile, and which are failing structurally. That data drives Days 18–20.

Days 18–20: Second Owner Accountability

If you have been running the system correctly since Day 11, at least one owner has missed their standard more than once. Days 18 through 20 are when you have the first formal accountability conversation.

This is not a coaching session, not a motivation talk, not a warning disguised as feedback. This is a direct exchange between a manager and an owner, with a documented record and a defined next step.

Structure the conversation using the Standard-Check-Consequence framework:

Step 1—State the Standard

Be specific. Read it from the written document. "The standard is [exact language]. You own this."

Step 2—Reference the Documented Misses

Not from memory. From the log. "On [date], the standard was missed. On [date], it was missed again. I addressed it both times." The documentation removes the argument about whether the misses happened.

Step 3—State the Consequence Clearly

This is the step most managers skip, and skipping it makes Step 2 meaningless. The consequence must be specific and it must happen. Not: "If this keeps happening, we'll have a problem." Specific: "If this standard is missed again, here is exactly what occurs." Name it. Then hold to it without modification.

Step 4—Define the Next Step

"The standard deadline is [time]. The next check is [time]. I will verify it personally." The conversation ends with a concrete and time-bound commitment, not with a general understanding that things need to improve.

What this conversation is not: It is not the place to explore the owner's motivations, revisit the fairness of the standard, or offer empathy for the difficulty of hitting the deadline. Those conversations have a place—but not here, not in an accountability exchange with a documented record of repeated misses. The time for coaching is before the pattern is established. By the second miss, you are not coaching. You are enforcing.

By Day 20, you have had at least one real accountability conversation. You have documented it. The system is no longer theoretical.

Phase 3—Days 21–30: Hand Off and Inspect

Phase 3 has a single strategic goal: make the system run without you standing over it. A system that requires your constant presence is not a system. It is supervision. The difference between the two is whether the operation holds when you step back. Phase 3 is the test of that.

Days 21–24: Secondary Leader Activation

Identify one person on your team who is ready to own the verification role—the pre-deadline checks—for at least two of your five standards. Ready does not mean perfect. It means they understand the standard, they can recognize a miss, and they will report what they find without filtering it to protect someone.

Have the handoff conversation with that person directly. The conversation has four components:

"I have been running this check. I want you to own it. Here is what the check looks at: [specific standard language and deadline]. Here is what you document: [format—time, status, any constraint observed]. Here is what you do if the answer is no: [specific escalation step—contact you immediately, log it, initiate the correction protocol]."

Do not generalize the handoff. Vague handoffs produce vague execution. The secondary leader needs to know exactly what they are looking for, exactly what they are writing down, and exactly what they do when the answer is wrong.

After the handoff, your role changes. You are no longer the person running the check. You are the person inspecting whether the check was run. This distinction is not semantic—it is the entire logic of building a management layer beneath you.

Do not inspect the standard directly. Inspect the secondary leader. Did they run the check? Did they document it in the format you specified? Did they escalate correctly when they found a miss? If yes—the system is transferring. If no—the handoff has a gap and you address it the same way you address any other miss: directly, immediately, and with documentation.

By Day 24, you have at least two standards being checked by someone other than you. You are verifying the verifier.

Days 25–27: System Documentation

Write down everything you built in the last 25 days. Not for a binder that lives in a drawer. For you—and for the operation's continuity.

This document is not a policy manual. Think of it as a functional record of the system as it currently exists—it contains exactly five sections:

Section 1: The 5 Standards

Full four-component version of each standard. Exact language. No abbreviations.

Section 2: Owners

One name per standard. Date they received the standard in a direct conversation.

Section 3: Check Schedule

For each standard: the check time, who runs it (you or secondary leader), and the documentation format.

Section 4: Consequence Protocol

For each standard: what the defined consequence is for a miss, and what the escalation path looks like after two documented misses.

Section 5: Secondary Leader Assignments

Which secondary leader owns which checks. The handoff date. What they are documenting and where.

This document is your system. If you were pulled out of the operation tomorrow and did not return for seven days, this document is what allows the operation to hold. If the operation would collapse without you present, this document either does not exist or was never operationalized. The goal by Day 27 is that both are false.

Days 28–30: The Test

On Day 28 or Day 29, step away from your operation for a full shift. Fully away. No check-ins. No texts asking how things are going. No quick walk-throughs at the midpoint. A full shift absent.

This is not reckless. You have spent 27 days building a system designed to run without you. If you do not test it, you do not know whether it is real.

When you return, do not ask how it went. Walk the operation. Answer the baseline questions from Before You Begin—the same five questions you started with on Day 1. What does the honest readout tell you?

Two Outcomes

Outcome 1: It Held

The standards were met. The checks were run. The documentation was completed. The secondary leader executed without escalating to you unnecessarily.

If this is the outcome: your system is real. Document what held and why—specifically. Which standards, which owners, which checks, and what the secondary leader did. This documentation is your proof of concept and the model you will replicate on the next set of operational gaps.

Outcome 2: It Broke

Something failed. A standard was missed and no one caught it. A check was not run. The secondary leader did not escalate when they should have.

If this is the outcome: that is not a failure of the 30-Day Plan. It is the data point that tells you exactly where the system is not yet built. Which standard? Which check? Which consequence? Go back to Phase 1 for that specific failure. Rewrite the standard if it was unclear. Reinstall the check if it was not running. Apply the consequence if it was not real.

The 30-Day cycle is not a one-time event. It is the model you run continuously on your weakest operational gaps. As the simpler problems are solved and held, you run the cycle on harder problems—cross-department coordination, multi-shift handoffs, coverage gaps, training failures. The methodology does not change. The problems get larger.

THE 30-DAY CYCLE

- Days 1–10: Write standards. Assign owners. Install checks. Minimum viable system.
- Days 11–20: Enforce on first miss. Document every outcome.
- Run pattern diagnostics. First accountability conversation.
- Days 21–30: Hand off checks to secondary leader.
- Document the system. Step away. Test.
- Day 31: Identify next operational gap. Start Phase 1 again.

This plan does not end on Day 30. Day 30 is a diagnostic, not a finish line. The System Commander does not complete a 30-Day Plan and move on—they complete a 30-Day cycle and begin the next one. The problems get harder. The system gets stronger. The operation holds because the manager built something that runs without constant presence, then built it again on the next gap, and the next. That is what command at scale looks like. Not heroic intervention. Not omnipresent supervision. A system that runs, checked by people trained to check it, enforced by a manager who acts on what they find. Run the cycle. Hold the standard. Start again.

LESSON

Day 30 is not the finish line. It is the diagnostic. The System Commander who runs the cycle once has built a system. The one who runs it again has built a habit. Run it until the habit outlasts your presence.

CHAPTER 20

The Leader You're Building Toward

> ***"The goal is not to be the best person on the floor. The goal is to build the floor that performs without you."***

It is 5:47 AM on a Tuesday. The parking lot is half-lit and quiet. The building is already running.

The freight finished at 4:20—twelve minutes ahead of standard. The opening checklist was completed and documented before the first customer arrived. The cooler temperatures are logged, in range, and signed off. At 6:03 AM, a coverage gap opened when a no-call came in for the first scheduled position on the floor. A secondary leader made the call, pulled from a float pool, and documented the adjustment. No one called. No one needed to. The honest readout—the one that doesn't soften anything—is clean.

The System Commander walks the floor. Not to find out what happened. To confirm what the system already reported. The walk takes eleven minutes. It ends at a desk where the previous night's check is documented and the current shift's check is in progress. There is nothing to react to. There is no fire.

This is not what Tuesday used to look like.

Tuesday used to start with a phone call in the car. Something broke overnight—freight did not finish, a standard was not met, a problem that should have been caught at midnight was not caught until 5 AM when the next person arrived and found it. The shift started in reaction. The first hour was triage. Whatever plan existed for the morning was deferred because the morning was already behind before it began. And underneath all of it was a familiar, exhausting awareness: the operation ran on one engine, and that engine was the person standing in the middle of it trying to hold everything together by will and presence alone.

That is not a staffing problem. Not a motivation problem. The root cause is a system problem—specifically, the absence of one.

What changed is not the team. The same people are working. They are not more talented, not more motivated by speeches or culture initiatives or a new set of values posted in the break room. What changed is that the system now tells them exactly what to do, when to do it, and what happens if it does not get done. A standard was written. An owner was assigned. A check was installed. A consequence was applied the first time it wasn't met, and the second time it wasn't met, and then it started being met. That sequence—written, owned, checked, applied—is the entire answer. There is no other answer.

The bench is built the same way. One developing leader. One system to own. Two weeks side-by-side. Then inspection, not management. Repeat. The operation now has three people who can run a system without being told to, two who are in development, and a leader who walks an eleven-minute floor check on Tuesday morning instead of spending the first hour in reaction.

To whoever is reading this from the middle of the version that is not working yet: the parking lot is still there. Every operation has one. It told you something this morning—either that the system held or that it did not. Not what you planned. Not what you intended. Not what you believe about your team or your leadership. What you allow—and what your system no longer permits.

You are not the mechanism. You were never supposed to be. The conversation you keep having—the same correction, the same reminder, the same explanation of what should already be understood—is not leadership. It is habit masquerading as a system. The goal of everything in this book is to make that conversation unnecessary. To build something that holds without you in the room.

When the system is built, the ritual goes quiet. The Tuesday morning check takes eleven minutes. It always does now. The readout is clean. That silence—not applause, not recognition, but an operation running exactly as designed—is the score.

That is the leader you are building toward. What comes next is everything required to build it.

> LESSON
>
> *The system is built in the moments you choose not to be the answer. Every time you hold back and let the structure respond, you build something that outlasts your presence.*

CORE TERMS

Glossary

The following terms appear throughout this book. Each one carries a specific operational meaning—not a general definition, but the precise definition used in the Command at Scale framework. Read them once before you begin. Return to them when a concept needs grounding.

System Commander

The leadership identity this book builds toward: an operations manager who runs the floor through a designed system rather than through personal presence and reactive intervention. A System Commander's operation performs consistently whether the leader is physically on the floor or not. The measure of a System Commander is not what they do when problems arise—it is how rarely problems arise because the system was built to prevent them.

Standard

A standard is not a preference, an expectation, or a goal. It is the specific, observable, measurable behavior or condition that defines acceptable performance, with a named owner and a defined time frame attached. A real standard can be checked by anyone with access to the floor—there is no ambiguity about whether it has been met. Anything that requires interpretation to assess is not a standard; it is a guideline.

The Control Test

A single diagnostic question: does your operation hold when you are not there? Not for an hour—for a full shift, for a week. The Control Test reveals whether a leader has built a system or built a dependency. If performance tracks the leader's physical presence, the leader is the system—and the operation is one absence away from failure at all times.

Standard-Check-Consequence

The three-part enforcement loop that makes a standard operational rather than theoretical. The standard defines the required condition. The check is the mechanism that detects deviation—scheduled, observable, and owned. The consequence is the defined response when the check fails, applied consistently regardless of who deviated or when. Remove any one of the three components and the loop breaks: the standard reverts to aspiration.

Three-Strike Rule

The accountability escalation framework for repeated standard failures. First deviation triggers a direct correction and documented coaching conversation. Second deviation triggers a formal performance discussion with a written improvement expectation. Third deviation triggers a consequence that the leader defined before the first miss occurred. The Three-Strike Rule works because the consequence is not invented at the third strike—it was established at the first, which removes ambiguity and makes the escalation sequence predictable for both parties.

Honest Readout

The visible gap between what a leader believes the standard is and what the operation is actually producing. Every operation carries an Honest Readout—it is readable on the floor, in the conditions, in the team's behavior when the leader is not present. The Honest Readout is not a management report. It is the physical state of the operation itself, which reflects not the standards that were written but the standards that were enforced.

The Hero Trap

The reward-architecture problem that keeps operations managers stuck in personal execution. The Hero Trap is activated every time a leader resolves a problem faster by doing it themselves than by training someone else to do it. Each personal intervention produces a short-term operational win and a long-term system failure—because it confirms to the team that escalation works, keeps the leader indispensable, and prevents the development of anyone who could absorb that category of problem independently. The trap is self-reinforcing: the more a leader rescues, the more rescue is required.

Bench Builder

The practice of deliberately developing at least one leader on the team who can replicate the system—not just follow it. A Bench Builder operates with explicit succession in mind: every standard they install, they teach. Every check they design, they train someone else to run. The Bench Builder's measure of success is not personal performance; it is whether the operation continues to perform when they step out of it.

System Commander Daily Audit

The five-question end-of-shift diagnostic that a System Commander runs against their own performance every day. The five questions: Did I enforce at least one standard today, immediately and without negotiation? Did I address any miss by changing the system—or did I simply repeat myself? Did I perform work today that belongs to the system, not to me? Did at least one team member solve a problem today without bringing it to me? If I had not been here today, what specifically would have broken—and why? Scoring is binary: a yes backed by a concrete example scores a 1, anything else scores a 0. Three consecutive days below 3 is a signal to rebuild, not to motivate.

WHAT COMES NEXT

Your Operation Will Not Fix Itself

I have watched a lot of leaders finish a book like this one. The ones who change something do it in the first seventy-two hours—before the operation pulls them back in and the urgency fades. The ones who don't change anything rarely go back.

If you want to move faster—if you want direct guidance, accountability, and a structured path to full operational command—the 12-Week Command at Scale Program was built for exactly where you are right now.

THE 12-WEEK COMMAND AT SCALE PROGRAM

- WHAT IT IS: A structured 12-week coaching program that walks you through installing a complete control system in your operation.
- WHO IT'S FOR: Operations managers, ops leaders, department heads, and multi-unit operators ready to build real control.
- WHAT YOU GET: Weekly frameworks, live coaching, accountability structure, and a peer group of leaders doing the same work.
- THE OUTCOME: In 12 weeks, your operation runs to standard without you living on the floor.

This is not a course you watch. It is a system you build—inside your actual operation, with your actual team, in real time. The leaders who go through this program do not just learn the system. They install it. They live it. And they finish knowing their operation will hold when they are not there.

> ***"You built the operation. Now build the system that runs it without you."***

APPENDIX A

The Control System Readiness Assessment

Use this assessment before beginning your first 30 days—and again at Day 30 to measure your progress. Score each statement honestly.

SCORING SCALE

1 = Almost never true 2 = Rarely true 3 = Sometimes true

4 = Usually true 5 = Consistently true

Section 1: Standards

1. My team can tell you the exact standard for each key process without asking me.	1—2—3—4—5
2. Standards in my operation are written down and visible—not just verbal.	1—2—3—4—5
3. When I observe a miss, I address it in the moment—not later.	1—2—3—4—5
4. My standards are specific and measurable. Done is binary.	1—2—3—4—5
5. I can identify the three most common misses in my operation right now.	1—2—3—4—5

Section 2: Ownership

6. Every critical process has one named owner—not "the team."	1—2—3—4—5
7. My team members know specifically what they own and what the standard is.	1—2—3—4—5

8. When a standard is missed, it is immediately clear whose responsibility it was.	1—2—3—4—5
9. I do not regularly step in and complete tasks that belong to someone else.	1—2—3—4—5
10. My team operates at or near full standard even when I am off the floor.	1—2—3—4—5

Section 3: Accountability

11. Missed standards in my operation have real, defined consequences.	1—2—3—4—5
12. I apply consequences consistently—not just when problems pile up.	1—2—3—4—5
13. My team does not need to be reminded of the same expectations week after week.	1—2—3—4—5
14. I close the loop after every correction—I confirm the standard was met.	1—2—3—4—5
15. I address accountability issues within minutes, not hours or days.	1—2—3—4—5

Section 4: Systems

16. I have checks built into my schedule that catch problems before they become habits.	1—2—3—4—5
17. When a problem repeats, I look first at the system—not just the person.	1—2—3—4—5
18. I have eliminated at least one recurring problem category in the last 90 days.	1—2—3—4—5
19. My operation has visible metrics the team can see without asking me.	1—2—3—4—5

20. I spend more time designing systems than fixing recurring problems.	1—2—3—4—5

Section 5: Scale and Bench

21. I am actively developing at least one person toward higher ownership.	1—2—3—4—5
22. My team leads operate with the same standard expectations I do.	1—2—3—4—5
23. If I left my operation for a full week, it would hold standard.	1—2—3—4—5
24. My supervisors can identify and address misses without waiting for me.	1—2—3—4—5
25. I measure my leadership by what holds in my absence, not what I do while present.	1—2—3—4—5

Scoring Guide

100-125	System Commander Your control system is installed. Focus on expansion and bench development.
75-99	Leader in Transition Strong foundation. Target your three lowest-scoring sections first.
50-74	Emerging Leader Real momentum building. Prioritize Standards and Accountability sections.
25-49	Operator Foundation stage. Start with your five biggest recurring misses immediately.
Under 25	Placeholder Mode This is the starting point—not the ending point. Start with Chapter 1. Now.

APPENDIX B

The 12-Week Command at Scale Program

Core Promise: In 12 weeks, you will install a control system so your operation runs to standard without you living on the floor.

Who It's For: Operations managers, ops leaders, department heads, franchise owners, and multi-unit operators ready to build real control.

This program is designed to be uncomfortable. Each week builds on the one before it, and if you skip ahead or treat any section as optional, you will feel the gap. This is not a motivational curriculum. It is a construction project. You are building a command system—one that survives your worst day, your highest-volume week, and the moment your best team member walks out the door. Commit to each week fully. Do the work before reading the next section. The twelve weeks here represent the operational spine of everything covered in this book, broken into executable units. Approach them the way you approach any high-stakes operation: with preparation, precision, and zero tolerance for drift.

This appendix contains Week 1 of the full program in its entirety. The complete 12-week build—Weeks 2 through 12, each with the same depth of frameworks, field notes, exercises, and Command Checkpoints—is available through the coaching program at commandatscale.com.

The twelve weeks begin with the question that underlies everything else: who are you actually functioning as right now?

Week 1—Identity: Operator, Leader, System Commander

Before you can build anything, you have to know what you are. Not what your title says. Not what your organization chart shows. What you actually function as—day to day, hour to hour, under pressure. When operations managers are finally honest about it, they discover they have been functioning primarily as Operators. They solve problems. They move inventory. They fill shifts. They do the work that needs to be done, and they do it faster than anyone else on the floor. This is not a small thing. The operational instinct that drives people into leadership roles is real, and it is valuable. But it is not sufficient.

There is a difference between being an Operator and being a Leader. An Operator executes. A Leader builds the conditions in which others execute consistently, without requiring the Leader's direct involvement in every decision. The gap between those two functions is the gap this entire program is designed to close. But it cannot be closed until you see it clearly—in yourself, not in your team.

The third identity—System Commander—is the one most leaders never reach. A System Commander does not just lead people. A System Commander engineers the environment in which performance either happens or does not, and holds that environment accountable. This is the hardest identity to inhabit because it requires you to trust structure over instinct, process over personality, and delayed measurement over immediate reaction. Having run a large-scale retail operation long enough to have seen every failure mode repeat itself, I can say with certainty that the leaders who plateau do so precisely at the transition between Leader and System Commander. They lead people well but never fully command the system. This week, you will identify exactly where you are sitting.

Week 1 is not about action. It is about honest diagnosis. The discomfort you feel doing the exercises below is data. Sit with it. Do not rush past it.

The Foundation Shift

Your identity drives your decisions before you are conscious of making them. If you identify primarily as an Operator, you will reach for solutions when you should be building systems. If you identify primarily as a Leader, you will reach for motivation when you should be enforcing standards. If you have never thought of yourself as a System Commander, you will not behave like one—because you cannot behave consistently as something you have not yet decided to be.

The shift from Operator to System Commander is not a promotion. It is a fundamental re-orientation of how you see your role. The System Commander's primary question is never "How do I fix this?" It is always "Why did the system allow this to happen, and how do I close that gap?" That question changes everything—what you pay attention to. What you document. What you tolerate and what you refuse to accept.

This Week's Work

1. THE IDENTITY AUDIT. For five consecutive days, keep a log of every significant decision or action you take during your operational shift. At the end of each day, label each item. Operator: you executed or solved. Leader: you directed, motivated, or coached a person. System Commander: you identified a structural gap and built or corrected a process. Do not adjust your behavior during the audit. You need accurate data, not a performance. At the end of five days, calculate the percentage of your time in each identity. Be prepared for the result to be uncomfortable.

2. THE ROLE ARCHAEOLOGY. Write a one-page honest description of how you actually spend your time—not how you think you should spend it, not how you describe your job in interviews. What are you actually doing in a typical eight-hour shift? Break it into approximate percentages. How much of it is physical execution? How much is directing people? How much is analyzing patterns and adjusting systems? This document becomes your baseline. You will revisit it in Week 12.

3. THE DECISION TRACE. Pick three operational problems that recurred in the last thirty days—issues you solved more than once. For each one, write: What was the problem? How did I solve it? Did my solution prevent recurrence, or did it only fix the instance? If you solved the same problem twice in thirty days, your solution was Operator-level. A System Commander's solution closes the door.

4. THE IDENTITY DECLARATION. Write a single paragraph—your operational identity statement—describing the kind of leader you are committed to being over the next twelve weeks. Be specific. Name what you will stop doing. Name what you will start building. This is not a mission statement. It is a contract with yourself. Keep it somewhere you will see it daily.

What to Expect

This week will feel abstract, especially if you are an action-oriented Operator. You will be tempted to skip the writing and go straight to doing. Resist that. The leaders who get the most out of Week 1 are the ones who slow down long enough to see themselves clearly. Expect some cognitive dissonance when your log reveals that you are spending the majority of your time as an Operator despite holding a leadership title. That dissonance is productive. It is the gap you are here to close. Success at the end of Week 1 looks like this: you have an honest picture of your current identity mix, and you have made a clear, written decision about what you are building toward.

Field Note

In my fifteenth year running operations, I pulled my logs from the previous quarter and looked at where my time had actually gone. I had convinced myself I was operating at a strategic level—coaching leaders, building systems, holding standards. My logs told a different story. Forty-two percent of my documented actions were Operator-level: I had restocked a section myself because it was faster, I had personally called a vendor because I knew the relationship, I had rearranged floor sets because I had not trusted the execution. None of those things were wrong in isolation. Collectively, they told me that I had been running the operation as an experienced Operator wearing a commander's title. That audit was the most useful hour I spent that entire year. It did not feel useful. It felt like a verdict.

WEEK 1 COMMAND CHECKPOINT

1. What percentage of your current daily activity is truly System Commander-level work?
2. Name one problem you solved in the last thirty days that you had already solved before. What does that tell you?
3. What operational decisions do you make by instinct that should instead be governed by a documented standard?
4. What would your operation look like if you were removed from it for two weeks? What would collapse, and why?
5. What specific belief or habit is keeping you in the Operator identity longer than your role requires?

What the Full Program Covers

Week 1 gives you the diagnostic. Weeks 2 through 12 give you the build. Each week installs a specific component of your control system—in sequence, in your actual operation, with your actual team. The full program is structured, accountable, and designed so that every week produces a tangible output you can see on the floor before you move to the next one.

Week	Focus	What You Build
2	Standards, Not Speeches	Written operational standards for your three highest-failure areas
3	The Repeating Miss	Root-cause analysis and structural close for your most recurring problem
4	Standard-Check-Consequence	A complete accountability loop for one critical standard
5	The Promotion Gap and the Hero Trap	A personal hero audit and a plan to exit Operator mode
6	Ownership: One Owner, One Standard	Single-owner accountability assignments across your operation

7	Clarity and Accountability	A closed-loop clarity-accountability architecture for your team
8	Accountability in the Moment	Scripted language and rehearsed delivery for real-time corrections
9	The Daily Audit	A five-question daily self-audit installed as a permanent habit
10	Command Across the Team	A culture-assessment tool and a plan to extend command below you
11	Mapping Your Control System	A full visual map of your control system and its weak points
12	Results, Reset, and Next 90 Days	A 90-day reset protocol and your next-level identity declaration

What you just read is Week 1. There are eleven more, each built to the same depth—a framework, a set of structured exercises, a field note from practice, and a Command Checkpoint that verifies the work is actually installed before you move on. Every week produces something tangible on your floor. By Week 12, you will have a complete control system running without you standing over it.

If you are ready to build the rest of it, the full program is waiting.

ACCESS THE FULL PROGRAM

The complete 12-Week Command at Scale Program—including all weekly frameworks, exercises, field notes, and Command Checkpoints—is available through the coaching program at:

commandatscale.com

APPENDIX C

The System Commander Creed

Print this. Post it where you will see it before every shift.

THE SYSTEM COMMANDER CREED

I set the standard.
I enforce the standard.
I never negotiate performance.

I rely on systems, not effort.
I move fast. I think clearly. I execute relentlessly.

I am a solution to a problem—not a title on a door.
I do not wait. I do not hope. I do not circle back.

When I see a miss, I address it now.
When I see a system failure, I fix the system.
When I develop a leader, I build someone who replaces my presence.

When I leave the floor, the system holds.

That is command. That is what I am.

I am a System Commander.

APPENDIX D

Laws of Command

These are the operating principles of the System Commander. Know them. Apply them. Teach them.

01	What you tolerate becomes the standard.
02	If behavior doesn't change, leadership didn't happen.
03	Repeated problems are not random—they are allowed.
04	Standards are enforced in moments, not meetings.
05	Repetition without consequence is noise.
06	Once—coincidence. Twice—pattern. Three times—it's a standard you tolerated into existence.
07	Clarity + accountability = control.
08	Delayed accountability is no accountability.
09	If it can be interpreted, it will be ignored.
10	Hero leaders get promoted and then trapped. System Commanders get promoted and then freed.
11	Shared ownership is no ownership.
12	If your team waits for you to show up before things get done, you've built a dependency—not a leadership system.
13	Design once. Enforce always.

14	Operators chase problems. System Commanders remove causes.
15	Control scales. Effort does not.

ABOUT THE AUTHOR

Michael Hollingsworth

Michael Hollingsworth is an operations leader with fifteen years of experience managing large-scale, high-volume retail operations. He has led hundreds of employees inside one of the country's most demanding operational environments—building systems that hold standard long after he leaves the floor.

His work has always been aimed at the same person: the operations manager who is excellent at their job and exhausted by it—who knows the operation depends on them too much and has not yet found a way to change that. Command at Scale is the framework he built to change it. Not in theory. In practice, inside real operations, with real teams, under real pressure.

Michael is the founder of Command at Scale, a coaching and leadership development platform built for operations managers who are ready to stop firefighting and start building permanent control in their organizations.

CONNECT WITH MICHAEL

- Website: commandatscale.com
- Coaching: 12-Week Command at Scale Program

COMMAND AT SCALE

Michael Hollingsworth

When you leave the floor, the system holds. That is command at scale.

www.ingramcontent.com/pod-product-compliance
Lightning Source LLC
LaVergne TN
LVHW011029110826
845149LV00015B/3339

* 9 7 9 8 9 9 5 8 8 4 2 0 0 *